Pastoral Care for Survivors of Family Abuse

Pastoral Care for Survivors of Family Abuse

James Leehan

Westminster/John Knox Press
Louisville, Kentucky

Scripture quotations from the Revised Standard Version of the Bible are copyrighted 1946, 1952, © 1971, 1973 by the Division of Christian Education of the National Council of the Churches of Christ in the U.S.A. and are used by permission.

Book design by Gene Harris

First edition

Published by Westminster/John Knox Press
Louisville, Kentucky

PRINTED IN THE UNITED STATES OF AMERICA

9 8 7 6 5 4 3 2 1

Library of Congress Cataloging-in-Publication Data

Leehan, James.
    Pastoral care for survivors of family abuse / James Leehan. — 1st ed.
        p.   cm.
    Bibliography: p.
    ISBN 0-664-25025-4

    1. Adult child abuse victims—Pastoral counseling of. 2. Abused women—Pastoral counseling of. 3. Family violence—Religious aspects—Christianity. I. Title.
BV4463.5.L44 1989
259—dc19   89-5441
                                                                CIP

I dedicate this book to all those who have worked
with Grown-Up Abused Children groups over the years,
especially my co-leaders

Elizabeth Carmichael

Christine Courtois

Laura Webb

Carol Tobin

Shela Perry Williams

and Maggie Jackson

who have given much time and supplied many insights.

And to my wife

Angie

whose understanding, love, and support have made
my work with survivors of family violence possible.

Contents

Preface and Acknowledgments

I do not usually ascribe events in my life to divine intervention. To claim that things I do or things that happen to me are "God's will"—much as I hope and pray they are—seems presumptuous. However, the fact that this book has come to be is an experience that was never part of my life's plan.

The original outline (which has been maintained with only minor changes) was scribbled out in one evening following a conference on "The Religious Community and Family Violence" in which I participated The discussions and conversations of that day generated a spontaneous list of issues that I felt should be better understood by pastors and religious counselors—maybe secular counselors as well. I do not normally think so clearly or completely late at night.

Even the signing of the contract with The Westminster Press for publication of the book seemed out of the ordinary. A few weeks after sending the outline to some publishers, I was to attend a National Campus Ministry Association conference in Philadelphia. As I was gathering my papers in preparation for leaving, I remembered that one of the publishing companies was in Philadelphia. I thought, I'll take my outline along and give them a call to see if they have any questions. A phone call early in the week resulted in meetings with the publisher and editorial director as well as other department heads, and by the time I left we had agreed on the terms of a contract. Even the publisher told me, "I want you to know, things don't normally happen so fast in this business."

Actually, my whole involvement in the area of family violence has been fortuitous. A chance conversation with a faculty member resulted in my first Grown-Up Abused Children group; a recommendation by another faculty member that a training manual originally designed to be mimeographed for group leaders be sent out for publication led to my first book in the area; a conversation with a student prompted the development of a course on Domestic Violence at Cleveland State University that is constantly oversubscribed. And now there is this book.

If God's will has been involved in this process, I wish God had been a little more active in the actual writing. Sometimes that became a real drag. But whatever God's role has been in this venture (and I leave that judgment up to you, if you care to make it), the end product is before you. I hope it will contribute to a better understanding of the physical, psychological, and spiritual needs of the many survivors of family abuse who are among the saints in the religious congregations in our society. Its goal is to instruct and inspire religious leaders of all faiths so that they will be more aware of the violence occurring in families, more responsive to the needs of the victims, and more committed to joining the struggle to end such abuse. That such a goal is the will of the God who "is peace" (Judg. 6:24) is one thing about which I am sure. If this book contributes to that goal, "I delight to do thy will, O my God; thy law is within my heart" (Ps. 40:8).

Although the outline for this book has not changed substantially, the title has. The original title was "Victims Among the Saints." Most of the people I first tried it with, family members, friends, and co-leaders of groups, thought it was good. However, when I shared it with persons who had been in Grown-Up Abused Children groups, their response was subdued. When I pursued this lack of enthusiasm, they said they didn't like being referred to as victims. The word made them feel weak and somehow deformed. Although they knew they had been victimized, they were struggling valiantly to stop being victims. However, they were not sure of what word to use instead.

For a time I worked without a title at all. Finally, further discussions resulted in the word "survivors." This represented a growth in my own awareness of the process people who suffer family violence must go through, and I thank those group members who made me aware of this by their gift of sensitivity.

All persons subjected to abuse are victimized by that process. Their sense of personal control, dignity, and worth are taken from them. They lose their sense of identity. Their personality has been distorted. Then, as these same persons free themselves from the control of their abusers, work to regain control over their lives, and affirm their dignity, worth, and identity, they reassert their own lives, their own existences. They become survivors. While it is true that for many the road to survival is long and arduous, they have at least begun the process of redefining their personalities separately from those of their abusers. The beginning is the most critical step. To continue to refer to such persons as victims is to deny the important process they have begun and the progress they are making.

I hope sharing this clarification in my own thinking also makes something clear to my readers. The people we are talking about in this book are not merely, or even primarily, persons who are presently experiencing abuse in their families. The principal focus of this book is on those persons who have experienced abuse in the past and are struggling to overcome its effects. These people may be adults who experienced abuse ten, fifteen, or twenty years ago and are still struggling to overcome the anger, confusion, and frustration that haunts their lives. They may also be battered women who are seeking outside help for the first time to break the cycle of violence that has terrorized their lives and those of their families. No matter how recently a person has experienced abuse, the fact that she or he is asking for help transforms this person from a victim into a survivor. The process of healing has begun.

It cannot be denied that many in our congregations are still silently suffering abuse. They need to be recognized and their needs met. Although such persons are not the primary focus of this book, much of what is discussed does apply to them and I have tried to make their plight clear. I also believe that pastors who become more sensitive to the survivors in their midst and who speak to their needs in sermons, seminars, and counseling will exhibit the pastoral and theological sensitivity that will inspire the victims among the saints in their congregations to become survivors.

Although this book is written primarily for persons involved in pastoral care in religious congregations, I hope it will have a broader application for social workers, educators, and all others involved in the helping professions, as well as any caring person interested in alleviating the anguish of those suffering from violence in their families. I also hope that those who are now experiencing or who have experienced abuse will find insights and inspiration in these pages to enrich their lives and free them from the pain of their past.

This book addresses four levels of response to the many survivors in our religious congregations. The first is that of recognition and understanding. Family violence is a difficult topic of conversation anywhere, but it is an especially sensitive one in religious communities. Because of this reticence the issue is seldom addressed, survivors as well as victims feel they cannot share their experiences, and their needs go unrecognized and unmet. Sometimes offhand comments or inadvertent remarks by pastors or church members tell victims and survivors that this is not a place to find understanding and support. Other times pastors and church members feel driven to distraction by the behavior of persons who have experienced abuse. A better understanding of the reasons for that behavior would make working with such people easier and more productive. This book should provide insights to enable religious leaders to be more sensitive and sympathetic and also to design programs that respond to the needs of victims and survivors alike.

The second level is theological. Too often, religious expressions and biblical passages are used to justify family violence. Some people working in the field even maintain that religious teachings *cause* family violence. Although I think such a position is too strong, I do believe some beliefs contribute to such violence and have been used to condone it. This book will examine some of those expressions and passages, offer alternate ways to understand them, and suggest ways that pastors might address the issue of family violence in their preaching and teaching.

A third manner in which pastors can respond to the survivors among their saints is that of spiritual direction, worship, and parish programs. What special spiritual problems exist for survivors? What forms of prayer and meditation can be helpful? Regarding worship, chapter 8 offers a sample service that was prepared here in Cleveland. Such a service could be used for Sunday worship or as a special commemoration of Victims' Rights Week or Child Abuse Prevention Month. We in the religious community must begin to use all our resources—spiritual as well as physical and financial—to bring an end to violence in our families.

Finally, for those pastors who provide in-depth counseling, I share some insights gained in ten years of working with grown-up abused children, both individually and in groups. I have made some mistakes that others can avoid, and I have identified some common themes, issues, and problems the recognition of which has made my work easier. I hope that by sharing them I can make the work of others easier too.

Many people have earned my gratitude for their help and support. Most important is my wife, Angie. She deserves a great vote of thanks not only for her encouragement and her willingness to read and offer suggestions on the manuscript but also for her forbearance for the many things that have not gotten done around home this past year. Thanks also to our daughters,

Barbara and Kathy, for their patience with my preoccupation with this project.

Many people have contributed ideas and insights. Laura Webb read the manuscript and offered suggestions. Maria Perusek researched statistics on family violence. Kathy Soltesz, the University Christian Movement secretary, put in extra time to listen to my mumbling into the dictaphone and transcribed a good part of the first draft. Cheryl Reade and Carol Reid shared insights from their spiritual struggles. Aggie Hoskins, Barbara Oehlberg, and Carolyn Olds Michels worked with me to prepare the worship service in chapter 8. The work of several Cleveland State University faculty members, and persons from the family violence services community of Cleveland who participated in the Domestic Violence course at CSU, helped me refine my own thinking, and I am grateful to Robert Wheeler (History), Ronald Reminich (Anthropology), Andrew Edwards (Social Services), Richard Yates (Counseling), Alice Walker (Psychology), Lydia Wochna (Cleveland Metro General Hospital, Social Services), Deborah Rex, Laurie Smith, and Rosemarie Heyer (Bellflower Center for the Prevention of Child Abuse), Anita Smith and Susan Petrarca (Women Together), Diana Cyganovich (Templum House), David Larson (Witness Victim Program), and Carolyn Sugiuchi (Cuyahoga County Adult Services Program).

I would be remiss if I did not also thank the members of my various Grown-Up Abused Children groups over the years. Their courage and commitment inspired me and strengthened my commitment to finish this book. I hope its publication will mean that fewer people will suffer the violence they experienced and that those who do suffer such abuse will find more sympathetic and informed assistance in their synagogues and churches.

1

The Crowd of Survivors Among Us

One would have to be living in a socially sanitized bubble not to realize that violence is all too prevalent in our families. Sensational cases are regularly reported in the media. TV docudramas examine the perils of battered wives. A close look at most violent crimes usually reveals the perpetrator to be a former victim of child abuse.

Even with all the reporting, only the most dramatic cases qualify for media coverage. With one out of twenty children experiencing abuse and fifty thousand wives battered annually— and those are only the reported cases—there would be little room for anything else if the newspapers tried to cover them all.

Family violence should be not merely a matter of media interest but also a subject of pastoral concern. Many cases never receive public notice or even attract the attention of the social welfare agencies designed to deal with the problem. There are also thousands of persons threatened and intimidated and children who are insulted, ridiculed, frightened, and neglected without a blow being struck. There is nothing specific to be reported, nothing concrete to be measured, and, since there is no evidence, statistically there is no abuse. But there is distress, pain, and anguish. Lives are distorted and crippled. Persons need consolation, support, and healing—things clergy are admirably trained to provide.

Clergy are also well positioned to respond to survivors of family violence. They are intimately involved with families, and they are often the first person family members turn to. Because of the nature of the suffering experienced and the distress caused, pastors are uniquely qualified to assist the survivors of family violence—those struggling to heal their deep scars. As the 1982 President's Task Force on Victims of Crime stated (p. 95):

> In hearing after hearing across the country, victims identified the religious community as a vital and largely untapped source of support for crime victims. The Government may compensate for economic loss; the state may punish; doctors may physically heal; but the lasting scars to spirit and faith are not so easily treated. Many victims question the faith they thought secure, or have no faith on which to rely. Frequently, ministers and their congregations can be a source of solace that no other sector of society can provide.

What crime victims are more deeply scared than those attacked in the "security" of their home by someone who professes "love"?

When we allow ourselves to think about the high level of violence in families, we realize there must be many instances in our congregations. We know there are victims, small children and adolescents who, as Margaret Hyde puts it so poignantly in her book title, "cry softly" over the pain they experience. There are grown women who were physically battered and are struggling to rebuild their lives. There are adults, both men and women, who experienced abuse as children and are now struggling to overcome the effects of that violence. Thousands of people are also co-afflicted. They were never abused, but they observed abuse in their families or are living with persons who are emotionally or psychologically handicapped because of the violence they experienced. Simple mathematics tells us that thousands of survivors of family violence exist in our society. They struggle with the effects of that violence even as they sit in the pews of our churches and synagogues.

These are not happy thoughts. They are not reflections one chooses willingly. But once they are considered we must ask pastoral questions: Who are these people? Where are they now? How do we recognize them? What pastoral responses are appropriate?

Statistics tell us that we don't have to look very far to find them. The past and present victims of family violence exist throughout our community. They are found in every stratum of society; they can be found in every educational and professional group. They can also be found in every religious congregation.

As we look at the people with whom we come in contact in our ministry, are we aware of the existence of survivors of abuse and are we sensitive to their needs? Do we know them when we see them? Do we know what to do when we recognize their existence among us? Do we know what difference their presence can or should make in our ministry? In most cases we have to answer no—despite the publicity now prevalent about family violence.

Few clergy or others in the caring professions in our society know how to respond to this problem. When we become aware of active cases of family violence we are uncomfortable. We feel that if we do anything we are intruding; we are interfering in a family matter. In most cases, all we do is report the incident to the appropriate agency, knowing with relief that we are fulfilling the requirements of the law. Then we let the authorities take over.

If we are aware that there are people in our congregations who have experienced abuse, we are not sure how to respond to them or what to say. Even if we acknowledge with them that this is part of their past, what difference does it make today? After all, it happened ten years ago. We, and often the victims themselves, prefer to think this is a matter of the past that is best forgotten. "Forgive and forget" is the byword. This is certainly not a matter for polite conversation. For most of us, family violence is something you read about but seldom have to confront directly. It is certainly not a major component of pastoral ministry.

This was certainly my attitude as a campus minister. I never expected to be involved with family violence, and certainly not with child abuse. I was dealing with a limited part of the population, those goal-oriented and highly motivated persons who become college students. The focus of my ministry was also to a restricted part of their lives, that of their work and study. I had minimal contact with their family relationships. I was involved with students as they struggled with the process of separation from their families—how to tell their parents they were changing their majors or planning to get married. Surely they were much too old for me to worry that they might be victims of abuse. I was involved in premarital counseling, but the possibility of violence in the relationship of two young people who were very much in love seemed far from the realm of possibility. Occasionally, I did get involved in marriage counseling when violence between partners had been an issue, but this was usually in the final stages of the dissolution of the marriage. I had little opportunity to identify cases of child abuse and certainly no direct contact with abused children. Little did I know!

Late in the fall of 1978, I became conscious that abused children exist even on a college campus. Elizabeth Carmichael, a faculty member in the Department of Social Services, shared with me the fact that she had recently taught a section on child abuse in one of her classes. A number of students had approached her privately to confide that they had been victims of child abuse. She was struck by the fact that each of them said they had never shared this experience with anyone before, and they each identified similar problems in their present life, problems that seemed to be connected to the fact that they had been abused.

Her account sparked memories of similar stories I had heard from some of my individual counselees. After several sessions they had shared with me the fact that they had been abused as children. They had revealed this information with some trepidation, because they had never talked about it before and felt they were betraying their parents. The kinds of problems that these students identified were similar to those shared by the social service students.

Elizabeth and I discussed our experiences at some length and determined that one of the major issues for these students was a profound sense of isolation. They had never told their stories before, and each felt that his or her problems were unique. Possibly, we concluded, they would receive some help from sharing their stories with one another. We contacted the students individually and asked if they would be willing to participate in such a group. Most, but not all, agreed to give it a try.

Early in January of 1979 the first Grown-Up Abused Children group convened at Cleveland State University. All present, including the leaders, were extremely nervous. What would happen? What would we talk about? We had agreed to meet for an hour and a half. Was there enough to fill the time? The first introductions were vague and general, but, as the more courageous of the group shared bits and pieces of their abusive pasts, the level of anxiety dropped and the students' eagerness to share with one another increased. Finally, they were with people who would believe their stories. Finally, there were people who understood what had happened, how terrible their childhoods had been, and what distress, confusion, anger, and frustration this abuse had created in their lives. These people would not challenge them to prove their stories. These people would not be horrified to hear their accounts of violence; in fact, they could match them story for story. It was finally all right to talk about what had happened. These people would listen and understand, believe and support them.

Two hours later we had to call the meeting to an end. In those two short hours a group had been born, and relationships established, in ways most of those present had never experienced. For the next seven months the group met faithfully every week. It was discontinued with great regret, but graduations and new jobs forced people to move in different directions.

Each year since then a similar group has met at Cleveland State

University. Minimal advertising produced more than the eight-person maximum for each group. After a few years, requests for memberships were received from the wider community. Volunteer leaders were recruited from the social service and mental health communities. Soon six to eight groups were meeting weekly throughout the greater Cleveland community. Unfortunately, an extensive waiting list of prospective members still exists.

The disquieting conclusion reached from all of this is that there are a tremendous number of survivors of family violence in our city—and Cleveland is hardly unique. There are persons living and working in cities and towns throughout this country who are carrying on normal lives, and being productive members of society, who are also living with the anguish of betrayed trust and lost childhoods. And they have no one with whom to share their pain. Many of those who have tried have been rebuffed—even by their pastors.

Over and over again in our groups, members have recounted, with furtive glances toward the clergy person present, their experiences when they tried to confide in their pastors. These experiences generally fell into two categories.

The first response was denial. If their efforts were made while they were still children living at home, the response was frequently, "But I know your family! Your father is a member of the vestry. He would not do the kinds of things you are describing. You are just an overly sensitive adolescent." In fairness, it should be noted that such responses came ten to fifteen years ago, before the issue of child abuse was widely recognized and discussed. There was even less information available then than there is today. Such responses were also common from teachers and school guidance counselors. It is entirely possible that the pastor's description was accurate; the child's parents may have been outstanding members of the congregation. That does not mean they were not abusing their child. Church involvement does not rule out abusive parenting practices.

One of my most disquieting experiences as a group leader came a year after a particular member had been in the group. A dinner was held on campus. Parents were invited. This former group member, gratefully now a more satisfied and productive student, made it a point to introduce me to her parents, both of whom had been abusive. Her parents were professional people, one a doctor, the other a lawyer. Both were active in their local church and had been involved in missionary efforts. I spent a very uncomfortable half hour talking with these "outstanding church leaders" whom I knew to have been very abusive as parents. We discussed a wide variety of mutual clergy contacts. The cognitive dissonance was overwhelming. It was not hard to understand how their daughter had been branded a rebellious adolescent when she sought help for the physical and sexual abuse that had been inflicted on her ten years before.

The second kind of response occurred when survivors tried to discuss the impact of past abuse on their present lives. In this area counselors, social workers, and psychologists have been equally at fault. Many group members reported that when they tried to discuss their abusive past as part of understanding their present dilemmas, they were rebuffed by both pastoral and secular counselors. The common response was, "That happened ten [fifteen] years ago. It's time to put it behind you and get on with your life. It has nothing to do with your present problems." Frequently the pastoral counselor would add, "You should forgive your parents for what they did to you. It is time to forgive and forget."

There is no question that grown-up abused children must get beyond their past, but not by denying it! And not by denying the fact that it has a profound impact on their present lives. They must recognize their abusive past for what it was—and still is—and give it its due as a significant part of their development, training, and present reality.

That such is the case should not come as a revelation to leaders of religious institutions, which are society's strongest advocates of family life. If religious institutions are willing to extol families as the basis for a sound society and the critical element for forming children, they must also be willing to admit that abusive families can and do create children with overwhelming problems. How a child is raised has important implications for how that child feels about herself or himself and how she or he behaves as an adult.

The maxim "Spare the rod and spoil the child," deduced from several sayings in the book of Proverbs, is commonly used to justify physical violence as a form of discipline. Although this issue will be discussed further in chapter 5, let us just say now that it certainly does not justify broken bones or life-threatening injuries. This maxim should be tempered by one from Paul's letter to the Ephesians, "Fathers, do not provoke your children to anger" (6:4). No biblical maxim should be applied outside the fundamental context of the scriptural story of a loving and caring God who is concerned for the welfare of all persons. An important part of that well-being is the message one internalizes about oneself. How a child is treated constitutes an important part of what that child learns and incorporates into his or her adult self-definition. Parents are very willing to take the credit when a child does well, but they are not always willing to look closely at their responsibility for a child who turns out badly or has difficulties as an adult. Then the child is just a bad apple or the black sheep of the family with whom no one could do anything.

It is true that one must be careful about making direct cause-and-effect connections in every case, but there is enough correlation between destructive and even criminal behavior and a previously abusive childhood to make one pause. The relationship appears frequently enough to prompt us at least to give the matter consideration.

This was brought home to me several years ago when I attended a conference in Chicago on child abuse. Since I was going to be in the city, I contacted a friend there who directs a drug treatment center and arranged to stay with him and his wife the night before the conference. During the course of our evening's conversation, he revealed that he was also planning to attend the conference. He explained his decision, "After you explained why you, as a campus minister, were coming to a conference on child abuse I looked into our client records. Seventy percent of our clients have identified themselves as growing up in abusive families! With that kind of statistic, someone in our agency should learn something about the dynamics of child abuse. . . . And now we can spend more time together."

The fact that 70 percent of the clients of a drug treatment program grew up in abusive families may be a surprising statistic, but unfortunately it is not uncommon. Although specific statistical correlations are hard to find, Steinmetz (1977) has gathered some data in this area. "In numerous studies of adolescents and adults who committed acts of criminal violence, brutal childrearing techniques and witnessing parental violence during childhood emerged as common early-childhood experience" (p. 102). One study found that nearly 70 percent of perpetrators of homicide "had a history of violent child rearing" (p. 103). Another study, of "wives who had experienced severe beatings from their husbands, found that half of the wives attempted suicide or self-mutilation" (p. 105). She offers a summary conclusion: "The more an individual is exposed to violence both as an observer and a victim during childhood, the more likely the individual is to be violent as an adult" (p. 105). The most disturbing form of that violence, of course, is another generation of child abuse. Some agencies report that as many as 90 percent of the abusive parents they treat were abused as children.

However, after citing all these statistics to support a cause-and-effect relationship between the experience of abuse and problems of later life, we must insert a word of caution. These statistics are gathered from only one end of the continuum. People who have problems are identified; then their past is studied and abuse is discovered. Not studied are all the people who were abused but are *not* destructive members of society. What about all the survivors of child abuse who have never been in jail, who use alcohol in moderation, and are caring and loving parents? These statistics are harder to come by.

Fortunately, Dr. Richard Gelles, one of the original researchers in the field of domestic violence, has conducted some studies in this area. In a talk he gave in Cleveland a few years ago, he reported tracking abused children into their adulthood and to the point to where they had their own families. Only 50 percent of them exhibited tendencies to be abusive. This is, of course, higher than the norm, but it is considerably better than the all too common misreading of the previous statistics, which imply that over 90 percent of formerly abused children are certain to abuse their own children. If that reading of the statistics were correct, there might be justification for legislating family planning practices for survivors of abuse. Fortunately, this is not necessary. I have found the grown-up abused children with whom I have dealt to be extremely conscientious and skilled parents.

It is clear that we must be careful how we use statistics. They can lead to the assumption that almost every abused child will grow up to become a drug addict, an abusive parent, or a Mafia hit man—or all of the above. Too much emphasis on such statistics simply conveys another negative message to grown-up abused children. It tells them that the painful experiences of their childhood and the denigrating messages they received are now carried to their ultimate conclusion: "Because of the experiences that made your childhood miserable, you are also condemned to fail as an adult." When such conclusions are too easily reached, there should be little wonder that survivors of abuse feel helpless and that their suicide rate is high.

What we do not know with all of the statistical information, even that of Richard Gelles, is what factors enable grown-up abused children to overcome the effects of their childhood and avoid behaving in ways that could be harmful to themselves and to others. It is my contention that not all survivors are destructive, but all have dysfunctional behavior patterns that make their lives painful and their relationships with others confused. Not all former survivors of child abuse are mentally ill, but all have gaps in their psychological development processes that interfere with personal performance and satisfaction. Not all adults abused as children have tendencies toward violence, but they have learned to deal with other people and with social situations in ways that are self-defeating and unproductive. Their abusive families taught them many effective ways to deal with an abusive and harmful environment. These methods are not effective in a broader world where most people are caring and supportive, but because these are the only methods they learned, they are the only interpersonal skills they have.

What grown-up abused children need is understanding and support as they try to understand their past. They need education and training so they can unlearn methods they know well but which are destructive and counterproductive. Then they can learn new ways to relate to people around them. To be more specific, they need to learn when to use the highly developed self-protection skills that were ingrained in them during their youth and when they can be open and trusting with those around them. In many ways, they need to get back in touch with their childhood in order to sort out what aspects of it are appropriate for the real world they live in today. In the words of Ray Helfer's book (1984), "childhood comes first," and many grown-up abused children need "a crash course in childhood for adults," (his subtitle) to learn the basic life skills they were never taught as children.

It is to this process and the role that ministers and rabbis can play in it that the rest of this book is dedicated. If we as religious leaders are willing to accept the fact that there is a crowd of survivors in our congregations, we must think carefully about who they are, what they need, and how we can best respond to them, both personally and through the institutions with which we work. We must determine how we can best be of service to these suffering ones.

2

What Happened to the Survivors Among Us?

What is the perfect family? Who has experienced a perfect childhood? Maybe some of you were paragons of virtue who never needed to be punished, who were never swatted or spanked, yelled at or ridiculed or reprimanded. Maybe some of you had perfect parents. They never got frustrated or out of sorts. They knew all the proper child-rearing techniques and practiced them perfectly. Maybe a hand was never raised in anger in your family and never a harsh or a discouraging word uttered—and for you the sky was not cloudy all day. If so, thank God, because you were uniquely blessed.

But if some of you were occasionally spanked, maybe even with a stick or a strap, or if you were berated and ridiculed for your adolescent foibles, were you then abused? Should you be examining your own life for signs of dysfunction and destructive behaviors? This is a question no author can answer in general terms for all readers. One must come to terms with one's own past, with one's own childhood—even in a family that was not abusive. All children must determine for themselves if and how the sins of their fathers are being visited upon them in their adulthood.

But the question remains: Who are the victims of abuse among us? Are they every child ever spanked? Or are they only those who required hospitalization? This is clearly an extended continuum. But even as we acknowledge that there are few accurate lines for determining when the discipline of a child, whether physical or verbal, becomes abusive, we must be careful not to justify corporal punishment too easily. All too often we spend more time in justifying traditional and physically violent methods of punishment than in seeking alternative nonviolent ways of discipline and training.

The question, When does physical violence become abuse? is frequently raised when I do workshops on domestic violence. On one occasion a woman who was a social worker was particularly insistent. For several minutes she pushed her point. "What are you calling abuse? How do you know when striking a child becomes abusive? What if you have an incorrigible child with whom there is nothing else to do? Reason has not worked. The only alternative is to beat him. What is wrong with that? It gets the message across. How do you know if it is abuse?"

In frustration I finally blurted out, "One way you might consider answering that question is to determine whether you would want whatever you are doing to the child done to you. Is it the way you would want to be treated?" Her vehement retort was, "But I am an adult!" The groans from around the room seemed universal. I could only answer, "If that's the determining factor, you have to decide why children deserve less respect than adults and then decide at what age they should be accorded the same rights as adults not to be physically beaten. That is a philosophical question. We do not have time to answer it today. We need to move on to other parts of the workshop." A few minutes later she slipped quietly out of the room.

This woman stated her case so starkly that she lost whatever support she may have had from others who thought that some level of violence should be acceptable as a means of disciplining difficult children. However, she did make explicit some of the unspoken assumptions of our society. Some things are allowed when dealing with children that are not okay for adults. Many things are acceptable within a family that would not be approved in the broader society. We have allowed double standards to exist in our approaches to child-rearing.

However, it is becoming increasingly evident that such approaches to child-rearing and family life are no longer adequate. Through psychology we have gained many important insights into the complex processes involved in the development of a healthy personality. As these processes become clearer we are learning how profound an impact the treatment we accord our children has on their later life. We must begin to look carefully at what we consider acceptable. We need to develop guidelines for how we treat our children that are clearer and more specific. We must find alternative nonviolent methods of discipline and training. We need to teach parents such methods.

We must also be willing to call certain forms of treatment abusive without obsessively branding every form of discipline as criminal. We must be willing to ask whether a particular form of treatment is harmful to the person being affected. For our purposes the key criterion for determining whether a behavior should be tagged abusive is: Is it harmful to the physical or emotional well-being and development of the person involved, whether that person is a child or an adult? To determine this we must take into account the many forms of abuse.

Although all forms of abuse are damaging, it is important to recognize that there are differences. Each form creates different personality and behavior dynamics. Each has different effects on later life and different impacts on the physical and emotional development of the persons experiencing them. The relationship of the abuser to the victim can affect the long-range impact of the violence. The age of the victim will determine the effects on a child's developmental processes. The forms of assistance and support available to the victim can influence the range, depth, and longevity of the impact.

All those factors can magnify or mitigate the psychological damage inflicted. Examining them would require many volumes. We will consider only the basic forms of abuse: physical, sexual, verbal, psychological, and emotional. We will also examine what might be called a more passive form of abuse, neglect.

Of course not all violence in a family is directed toward the children. There is also violence between the adult members of the family. The most common forms are the battering of wives and of elders. Sibling violence is also prevalent and is, in fact, the "most common form of family violence" (Gelles and Cornell 1985: 85). We will consider these separately at the end of this chapter.

Physical Abuse

Physical abuse involves the striking of a child by parents or caregivers. On the continuum already identified, it ranges from a mild swat on the behind, intended to get the child's attention, through a much more violent swat that leaves a bruise, to beatings that break bones and endanger life. The gentle swat may startle more than harm and may have little long-range impact beyond the gaining of attention that was sought. Bruises and broken bones clearly are harmful. However, we need to ask, is that really the extent of the damage?

Doris Bettes has written a moving short story which raises just this question. (I had the privilege of hearing Ms. Bettes read this story at a Campus Ministry conference.) The story is about an infant in a small southern town who is severely beaten by her father, who also kills her mother. The father is imprisoned, and another family takes the baby girl in as their own daughter. No one in town tells her about her real father and what he did, but everyone knows that someday he will return. Even though her bruises and broken bones have healed and the little girl was too young to remember what happened to her, everyone in town wonders, "Do the bones remember?" Do other effects remain after the bones have mended?

Judging by my experience after ten years of counseling with grown-up abused children, I'd say the answer is yes! Broken bones may heal and actually become stronger at the point of the break, but the crushing of the spirit that accompanies the physical damage heals neither so easily nor so well. Negative messages attached to the beatings remain for a lifetime to undermine the person's self-esteem and ability to trust another human being. This kind of harm requires a totally different kind of treatment —a treatment that often takes a long time and can itself be painful.

However, it was the recognition on the part of emergency-room doctors that the bones of some children had been broken repeatedly and in unusual ways that led to the present awareness of the extensiveness of child abuse in our society. Alert doctors began to realize that certain childhood injuries were occurring in unusual forms and in patterns too consistent to be accidental. Their reports to child welfare agencies revealed the frightening pervasiveness of the violence being done to children.

Physical abuse of this kind is the easiest to identify. It is also the most commonly reported because broken bones and multiple bruises are easy to verify.

Not all physical abuse results in a visit to an emergency room, and bones do not have to be broken to have something to "remember." Many children are slapped, punched, and even thrown across the room without sustaining an injury requiring medical treatment. But such children are certainly harmed, their physical well-being damaged, and their sense of security threatened, not only for this moment but for the foreseeable future. Even when they are too young to articulate them, the questions remain. "When will this happen again? What did I do to deserve it? What must I do to avoid it in future?"

To consider the impact of this treatment on the child's emotional development, one need only realize that for such a child the physiological need for safety is not being met. This need is identified by Abraham Maslow as the second in his hierarchy of needs, emerging as soon as the need for food is satisfied. Maslow (1987: 15–23) maintains that satisfactory fulfillment of this need is essential before a person can move on to fill other needs and develop other aspects of the personality. If one lives in constant fear for one's safety, little energy or attention can be directed to the pursuit of higher, more fulfilling goals of belonging, love, and self-esteem. One's personality development is thereby stunted.

Sexual Abuse

Sexual abuse involves any kind of sexual contact between a child and another person who has some form of authority over that child. Most commonly that person is a parent, but it may also be an older sibling, an uncle or aunt, a stepfather or stepmother, a grandparent, or a babysitter or trusted neighbor. The abuser may be of the same or different sex as the child. The abuse may take the form of touching, fondling, or sexual intercourse. The critical issue is that some form of sexual contact is imposed by someone responsible for the care and protection of the child and with whom such contact is considered socially inappropriate because of age difference or family relationship.

This sexual imposition may or may not involve physical violence. If the physical act is accompanied by violent force, the child experiences the dual abuse of physical pain and sexual exploitation. The child now feels not only physically attacked but violated in the most intimate way possible. The confusion that ensues is doubly agonizing. "Maybe my father hits me because I failed to clean my room or I said something wrong. But why is my father doing this shameful thing to me? What did I do to deserve this? What kind of terrible person must I be?"

Often the trusted authority figure does not force the child into sexual activity. He cajoles, tricks, or kindly manipulates the child into a sexual relationship. The child is convinced that such contact is okay. It is "what you do to be nice to your uncle."

But another message is added soon after the act is performed. "This is something just between us. This is not something we want to tell anyone else. It is our little secret." Although the act was supposedly good before it happened, it is clearly wrong after the fact. Even before the child is old enough to explain why, he or she knows something is wrong. It should not be told to others. It is something to hide and be ashamed of.

When the child learns the social taboos that are associated with such actions, the child's sense of shame and need for secrecy increases. A sense of horror and revulsion develops. The child feels betrayed and violated psychologically as well as physically. The special trust that existed between child and caregiver has been destroyed.

Sexual abuse may also be committed by a total stranger. As

harmful as that may be, the impact is not the same. Although the child's body is equally violated, the sense of betrayal is not as great. The level of social shame and disgrace is less. Such a sexual imposition has not entailed the same breaking of trust and the same failure of care and protection as there would be if the perpetrator had been a supposedly loving member of the family.

The betrayal of a loving and protecting relationship is an important aspect of the dynamic involved in sexual abuse. Not only does sexual abuse destroy the caring and protective relationship between child and adult, it also breaks down the whole system of care and protection within the family. The victim cannot help but wonder, if only subconsciously, why other members of the family did not interfere. "Even if my father was doing such an evil thing, why didn't my mother stop him? Didn't she suspect? Doesn't she care enough about me? Am I so evil? Didn't she think I was worth the effort?" Once again the child internalizes a whole series of negative messages.

The victim of sexual abuse is often faced with other internal conflicts. As he or she becomes more and more horrified and disgusted by what was done and by the manner in which the natural childhood desire to please and to be affectionate and caring has been exploited and manipulated, the child will ask, "Why didn't I stop it? Why didn't I tell someone?" The child will assume the blame for not stopping the relationship, for not telling someone. Thus mired in shame and guilt, the child will be unable to acknowledge what he or she really knows: that a child does not have the physical or emotional strength to stop abuse and there really is no one to tell. If other members of the family are willing to ignore what was happening or are not psychologically strong enough or emotionally independent enough to force the abuser to stop, the reality is that the child had no way to stop the abuse and no one to turn to for help.

If the sexual abuse was not violent, these grown-up abused children may also be aware that they experienced pleasure from the sex act. This further horrifies, disgusts, and shames them. "How could I enjoy something so revolting? What must be wrong with me if I can take pleasure from this?" Once again the quagmire of guilt and shame wipes out the rational recognition that such sensations are involuntary physiological responses and are something over which they do not have control.

Therefore, it should be evident that sexual abuse not only violates the rights of the child to bodily integrity but also inflicts severe mental and emotional anguish. Whether or not the sexual abuse is accompanied by violence, the victims receive the message that they are not important persons with valued rights. They learn that they are not worth protecting and are only objects for other people's pleasure. The children are inculcated with an intense sense of degradation and depravity as well as deep feelings of disgust for and yet preoccupation with sex. They experience profound confusion over their own sexuality and the role of sex as an appropriate expression of affection.

Verbal Abuse

Physical and sexual abuse are the most commonly identified forms of abuse. They constitute the cases most frequently reported to and investigated by child welfare agencies. Their immediate effects can be documented and judged. However, it should be evident from the discussion of both forms of abuse that the immediate physical effects are only part of the damage done. Many other harmful and damaging messages are transmitted that are usually more lasting than the physical pain.

However, these same messages can often be transmitted without a hand ever touching the child. Of such is the stuff of verbal abuse. Verbal abuse is the regular and consistent verbal denigration and belittling of a child by an authority figure responsible for the care and development of that child. It can involve explicit insults, name-calling, and put-downs. It can entail rejection or denial of successes and accomplishments.

Such abuse cannot be measured or documented. It is not a matter for court cases and newspaper stories, but it is just as devastating. My experience with grown-up abused children has prompted me to revise the childhood retort used with such comfort during childhood name-calling battles, "Sticks and stones may break my bones, but names will never hurt me." The saying may still be true when dealing with words coming from a childhood antagonist, but when the words come from the lips of a parental caregiver, perhaps from the mother who is supposed to love you, the words can forever hurt. It is in this context that the lines of Psalm 55:12–13 come to life:

> It is not an enemy who taunts me—
> then I could bear it;
> it is not an adversary who deals insolently with me—
> then I could hide from them.
> But it is you, my equal,
> my companion, my familiar friend.

As the psalmist eloquently tells us, messages from such sources strike us deeply. They remain long after physical bruises have healed. These messages create deep wounds that become infected with malicious cancers of self-doubt, fear, insecurity, and a profound sense of helplessness and worthlessness. Such wounds do not heal naturally and simply over time. They must be cut into, examined, and cauterized by a long and often painful process of identifying, probing, and confronting the multitude of negative messages internalized over the years. Even after being cauterized such wounds will not heal without ample doses of the caring and supportive ointment that was so lacking in the person's childhood.

Psychological Abuse

It should be clear by now that all abuse has psychological dimensions. These dimensions are the most long-lasting and the most difficult of all the effects of abuse to identify and to treat. However, abuse can also be primarily and even exclusively psychological. It may involve little or no physical contact and may not be physically violent. Such abuse may be inflicted without words and without any blows that could leave visible marks. Its wounds are on the spirit and psyche of the person being threatened and denigrated. Psychological abuse consists in the regular and consistent efforts of a caregiver to denigrate, control, or intimidate a child by fear, mocking, isolation, or spoken or unspoken threats.

Garbarino and Gilliam (1980: 74–75) identify four aspects of psychological abuse:

1. *Punishing positive, operant behaviors* such as smiling, mobility, exploration, vocalization, and manipulation of objects.

2. *Discouraging caregiver-infant attachment.* Such attachment is critical for child development, and its disruption can have profound effects.

3. *Punishing self-esteem.* To discourage self-esteem attacks a fundamental component of a person's development.

4. *Punishing interpersonal skills necessary for adequate performance in nonfamilial contexts* such as schools and peer groups.

Children are by their nature dependent. In order to survive and thrive they need regular care and nurture as well as adequate food, clothing, and shelter. As well as their minds and bodies, their characters and personalities are in the process of formation. They are highly susceptible to forces around them. They know they are dependent and have few, if any, resources outside their families. So when a child is paraded naked before snickering visitors, is not allowed to play with other children, is locked in a closet for long periods of time, is forced to watch pets or property being destroyed, or is threatened with being given or sold to an unsavory relative or neighbor, the child has little or no choice but to submit to the ridicule and intimidation. Such a child has little alternative but to live in constant dread and accept such conditions as a "normal" way of life. Although no blow may ever be inflicted, such children live in fear that they may be·the next victim of the same violence that destroyed their beloved pet. Even though no specific insult is uttered, their opportunities for personal development are severely hampered.

Sometimes such intimidation is experienced when children watch one parent beat the other. They wonder, "Will I be the next object of this anger? What will become of me if he kills her? What will happen to me if they separate? Is all this fighting my fault? What did I do wrong?" Such thoughts may or may not be the result of specific remarks by either parent, but the emotional distress is nonetheless real. The pain of the moment is no less intense and the psychological wounds are no less deep. The same negative messages are as deeply imbedded in the minds and hearts of these children as if they had been accompanied by violence. The messages continue into adulthood to taint their view of themselves and of other people around them. They find it difficult to feel good about themselves or trust others.

Neglect

The forms of abuse we have discussed thus far are all active ones, no matter how subtly they may be expressed. They all involve the utterance of a word or the commission of a deed of a hurtful nature. Neglect, on the other hand, is indirect. The abuse is not inflicted by words or deeds but rather by means of words not spoken and deeds not performed. A child is harmed because caring words are never spoken, because food, clothing, and shelter are not provided, because signs of affection are never offered. Neglect is the failure of caregivers either to provide for the physical and health needs of the children under their care or to meet the children's emotional, affectionate, or support needs.

Physical neglect is sometimes discovered in hospital emergency rooms when a child is brought in suffering from malnutrition or a disease resulting from unsanitary living conditions. A child may also be suffering from simple childhood diseases that have been allowed to progress to dangerous levels. Neglect may also be identified when a neighbor discovers that a small child is being left alone for long periods of time. No children should be left to fend for themselves at an age when they do not have the capacity to provide for their own well-being or to protect themselves from harm. When such cases are discovered, child welfare agencies are called to investigate. If the situation appears to be chronic, the agency may instruct the parents on how to provide proper care for their child. If such interventions do not solve the problem, the agency may remove the child from the home.

Neglect may also take a purely emotional form when parents fail to provide adequate affection for their children. Emotional neglect is only rarely seen in medical facilities. One way that such neglect has been discovered in a medical setting is when an infant is brought in who is failing to grow and to develop. This "failure to thrive" is a medical diagnosis often associated with the fact that a child has not received adequate human contact. The infant has enough food but has not been held, hugged, or cuddled enough to fulfill its emotional needs. The child's body fails to grow because it is starved for human affection. No matter how much food is available, the child is too emotionally and physically listless to take advantage of it. Such a child can in fact die from a lack of adequate human affection. The most effective form of medical treatment for such children is simply that they be held and hugged while being fed.

Most emotional neglect does not have dramatic physical impact. As neglected children grow older they learn to adapt to lack of physical contact. They come to expect that their mother will not touch them, will seldom speak to them, and will ignore them for long periods of time. Such children accommodate to their lack of emotional nurturing by becoming cold and distant and even hostile as they learn that the world is a cold, distant, and hostile place.

Emotional neglect often results from the parents' inability to provide for their own needs, let alone those of a child. The parent is sick or depressed and is unable to function in a caring or supportive way. In such a family, the children are forced to take care of themselves in ways far beyond the skills appropriate to their age. A five-year-old cares for younger siblings. A seven-year-old cooks for a family of six. A teenager is responsible for filling out Aid for Dependent Children forms and negotiating with welfare agencies for family support. Such responsibilities strain the emotional capacities of these children. Even as they "perform their tasks well," the toll taken on their emotional development is devastating. They feel emotionally empty and barren.

In such families the children are, in effect, taking over the roles of their parents. They end up fulfilling many of the caregiver roles that are more appropriately the parent's responsibilities. Often the roles the children perform are not merely those of the physical caregiver. They also become responsible for the emotional care and nurturing of their parents. Because Mother is "feeling poorly" they must soothe and care for her. Because Daddy is drunk so often he cannot be a supportive partner to his wife, the young child must take on the role of mature companion. For children growing up in such circumstances, the family is not a place "for cooperative mutual support and affection but for exploitation and the satisfaction of neurotic needs" (Justice and Justice 1976:70). In such families the children's needs are seldom met. They are left emotionally starved.

A survivor's hunger for emotional support was poigantly exhibited during one of our Grown-Up Abused Children groups. The group had been meeting for several weeks when a young woman came in, clutching a copy of a magazine article. She was visibly anxious throughout the meeting but refused to share the source of her anxiety. Finally, as the meeting neared its end, she gathered her courage and spoke in a voice that was as demanding as it was anxious, "This article says that everyone needs six hugs a day for their mental health. And I want mine! I figure that because of my family life I'm thousands of hugs behind. I want a hug from everyone here before we leave today!"

The group members were startled but responsive. They all both feared and hungered for such human contact. For some, human touching was unknown; for others, it had only been a source of pain. All were anxious to learn what gentle caring contact could be like in their lives. Everyone exchanged hugs at the end of that meeting. Someone suggested we do it again at the next meeting, and it became the ritual conclusion for every meeting. In some fashion, that same question has come up in every group and some method for exchanging hugs is devised. The group provides the supportive, caring environment never available in their families. It becomes one of the major sources for the emotional nurture of the members.

Battering

Another form of family violence common in our society is that occurring between adult partners in a relationship. Although the most common form is that of husbands battering their wives, women are also known to have struck and harmed their husbands. However, the violence initiated by husbands is usually more serious because men are generally larger and stronger than women and are able to do more harm. Men also seem to be physically more able and culturally more inclined to resort to violence. Reported cases of battered husbands are minuscule compared to those of battered wives.

Before discussing the dynamics involved in violence between adults, let me remind the reader of what was previously said about the psychological abuse inflicted on children when parents attack one another. Fear and anxiety pervade the lives of these children, coloring their images and expectations of family life, marriage, and the nature of relations between men and women.

At first glance, the dynamics of adults attacking one another would seem to be significantly different from those involved when adults abuse children. In the first place, a different relationship exists. The level of dependency and helplessness on the part of a battered wife is not nearly so extensive as that of a minor child. A wife supposedly has more options and more avenues of escape. She should be able to get out of the situation.

This, however, is one of the constant anomalies for those working with battered women. The woman seems to be as dependent and helpless as any child when it comes to trying to separate from her battering husband. She feels too worthless and ineffective to make a substantial move away from her violent situation. In some cases the woman is convinced her battering is a punishment she deserves. She believes she has no one to turn to for help and no way to break the cycle. She is as emotionally locked into the situation as a child who is physically dependent upon the family.

Because these similarities between the emotional limitations experienced by battered wives and the physical circumstances of abused children are significant, I will identify some of the points of connection and similarity between spousal battering and the abuse of children.

A strong statistical correlation exists between violence among marriage partners and abuse in those partners' childhoods. Richard Gelles (1979:101) cites several studies that support the assumption that "the more individuals are exposed to violence as children [both as observers and victims], the more they are violent as adults. . . . Violence can provide a role model for the offender, . . . it can also provide a role model for the victim. . . . The more frequently a woman was struck by her parents, the more likely she was to grow up and be struck by her husband."

Several explanations are possible regarding this correlation. Certainly, children growing up in such environments have learned that violence is an acceptable, if unpleasant, method for handling problems. Violence may not have been effective for solving problems, but it was the method regularly used. It is the technique most familiar to such persons.

Even if a child comes to the realization that violence is not the best way to resolve difficulties, he or she never sees or hears any other method. Without other models of interpersonal skills, when conflict arises in the grown-up child's own family, he or she will fall back on violence as a form of response because there do not seem to be any other options.

Another relationship between spousal battering and child abuse is that the personality traits and character patterns of the person being battered are almost identical with those we shall discuss in the next chapter as the recurring problems of grown-up abused children. Battered wives (as the most frequent victims, they are the most thoroughly studied) are identified as having low self-esteem and a poor self-image, a pervasive sense of helplessness, and an inability to make decisions. They are also generally isolated from other people and have few friends. These characteristics have been commonly diagnosed as "battered women's syndrome." They exist almost universally in women who are battered.

Given the high percentage of battered women who are also grown-up abused children, one might ask where the syndrome came from. Are the reactions of the victim-wife simply those learned in childhood? If that is their source, shouldn't that influence our way of understanding the problem and our approach to treatment? Might it not be helpful to the battered wife if she could understand that much of her present problem is the result of behaviors she learned as a child? If she learned those behaviors, she can unlearn them and learn new ones. The process of change may be difficult and time-consuming, but she is not locked in a hopeless cycle.

A similar observation can be made and a similar question asked about abusive parents. As we noted in chapter 1, some agencies estimate that over 90 percent of abusive parents were themselves abused as children. When one considers such statistics and also looks at the personality profiles usually attributed to abusive parents—isolation, low self-esteem, poor social skills, and a sense of helplessness—one wonders about the origin of such traits.

Sibling Abuse

Violence between siblings is extremely common and widely accepted as "part of growing up." It is thought by many to be a normal part of a child's learning process. Through fights with brothers and sisters, a child "learns to take it," learns how to survive in a competitive world. Such violence is so commonly accepted that researchers have found it difficult to study. Parents do not consider what their children are doing to be uncommon enough to report.

Sibling violence varies considerably depending on the age and sex of the children and also on variations in age and sex between the children involved. If one of the children is considerably older, any physical or sexual abuse can have an impact similar to that experienced if a parent were the offender. In addition, the abused child may wonder why the parents allowed it to happen and may develop considerable anger about their failure to provide protection.

Even if children are close in age, parental acceptance of sibling violence teaches children that violence is an approved way to solve problems. If, as often happens, one of the children becomes the family scapegoat, that child learns messages of inferiority and comes to believe that the parents are uncaring. All such messages have negative impacts on a child's development.

Elder Abuse

Although abuse toward adults can take different forms— parents who abuse their adult children, or adolescent and adult children who beat their parents—the abuse of elderly persons is particularly devastating because of their vulnerable position. This matter demands increasing consideration as the demographics of our society change. I will restrict myself to identifying the unique forms that elder abuse can take.

Abuse of the elderly can take many of the same physical and mental forms as that inflicted on children. Because of their physical vulnerability, older adults can be subject to much of the same injury, punishment, and intimidation as small children. It is also possible for them to be unreasonably confined or restricted in their contacts with others. Because older adults may have valuable personal resources, they may be exploited by their children or caregivers. These resources—money, home, or other property —may be unlawfully or improperly appropriated by others.

Such exploitation is specifically condemned by elder abuse laws. Laws on elder abuse also point out that older adults, like small children, can be neglected. Because of physical needs that may result from infirmity, the failure to provide things like medication, housekeeping, and personal care assistance can produce physical harm, mental anguish, or even mental illness.

Older persons who are abused are often as limited in their options as children. They are vulnerable and dependent because of illness or lack of resources. Often they are more cut off from society than children. Their peers to whom they might turn for assistance may be equally dependent, if they are still alive. There is no social institution, such as a school, to which they are expected to relate and from which they might expect help. To seek assistance they must admit that they raised a child who is capable of such behavior. If they seek relief, they are often branded as a "nasty, unappreciative old so-and-so." With such forces at work, it is small wonder that older persons who are being abused often report many of the same problems as grown-up abused children—isolation, low self-esteem, depression, and helplessness.

On that note, it is now time to look further at the nature of the survivors among us. We have considered what happened to them, the forms of abuse to which they may have been subjected. Now let us consider what they learned as a result of those experiences.

3

What Have
the Survivors Learned?

Families are the training grounds for society's children. Child psychologists maintain that the first four years of life are the most significant for character formation. What happens in the family is the single most important determinant of what a child does and becomes in later life. In families, basic human needs are met. In families, the first developmental crises that shape our personalities are resolved. What happens when these needs are not met, when these crises go unresolved or are resolved in negative or harmful ways?

Volumes of studies tell us that many families are not healthy or safe places for children to grow up. In fact, because of their families, many children do not live long enough to reach adulthood. The number one cause of death for children under age five is family violence.

Fortunately, however, most abused children are not killed. They live to become adults. But what about those abused children who are fortunate enough to survive? How do they live? What are their personalities like? What problems and anxieties do they face? What are their needs, and what kinds of challenges and responsibilities do they present to us as pastors and counselors?

When Elizabeth Carmichael and I formed the first Grown-Up Abused Children group, we were only vaguely aware that the students with whom we had talked had similar problems. We knew they all felt isolated, but we did not understand the exact nature of the problems they had experienced. Neither did we understand the connections between their present problems and their past abuse. All we knew was that they felt alone and they had been abused. Was a support group a good treatment method?

We were only guessing. What dynamics would develop when we brought together a group of students with similar family backgrounds? We really didn't know.

More inclined to foolishness than bravery and guided more by the Spirit than our combined knowledge of counseling and psychology, we simply jumped into the task. Generally speaking, the first group went well. Sometimes it floundered, other times the members blossomed through new insights and growth, but always the group continued to meet. In fact, we had to beg them to take a break. Frequently, we met together as leaders to discuss and try to analyze what was happening. Gradually we became clearer and more adept at what we were doing, and our confidence increased.

This process continued for me with a number of co-leaders. After Elizabeth left the university, Christine Courtois worked with me for the year before she left the university, and finally Laura Webb had the stamina (or was it patience?) to put up with me for several years. All of us analyzed what we saw happening. We identified patterns within the problems we were encountering. We noted connections between behaviors and relationships between present problems and past experiences. We identified major problem areas. When the Grown-Up Abused Children program began to expand in Cleveland and new leaders needed to be trained, Laura and I were forced to define and record our reflections.

The problem areas we identified are not unique to survivors of abuse. They are, in fact, areas where all people who are struggling for optimum development of their personalities may have problems or may desire greater maturity. However, for grown-up abused children the problems that arise are not merely a matter of living a fuller life or fine-tuning their sensitivities or more fully developing their human potential. The problems stem from a lack of basic skills or from enormous gaps in their experience or from paralyzing fears related to basic, simple human-relations tasks. The depth, intensity, and magnitude of the problems are substantially different. Because survivors experience many of them together, they constitute qualitatively different kinds of problems.

The list of traits that we developed is not necessarily the only way to categorize the problems of grown-up abused children. Nor is it exclusively applicable to them. Ray Helfer (1984:33–79) describes a World of Abnormal Rearing or "W.A.R. Cycle," which applies to many adults who missed out on their childhood. Lenore Walker (1979:31, 36, 254) identifies similar problems for battered women and their batterers. Our list is, however, a good analytical starting point for understanding the problems of the survivors among us, no matter what form of family violence they suffered.

It is important for pastors, even those not deeply involved with counseling, to understand the behaviors of persons who experienced family violence. Such knowledge will help pastors recognize the survivors present in their own congregations and be more sensitive to their problems and needs. They will then be able to offer appropriate help and referral.

Pastors need to be alert to these signs because few survivors are likely to identify themselves as such. Many are not willing to call what happened to them "abuse"; to do so raises too many painful memories they have labored long and hard to erase. To do so creates too much guilt because they feel they are betraying their parents; it also generates too much anxiety about how others might perceive them.

Other survivors may not even be able to identify their childhoods as abusive. They cannot let themselves acknowledge the reality of what happened. Still others may have totally blocked the experience from their memory. Frequently, grown-up abused children, even those who remember and admit what happened to them, have long periods in their lives (even several years) for which they have no recollections. Certain aspects of their abusive backgrounds are too painful. They block their memories as a method of self-preservation, as a way to maintain a semblance of normalcy in their lives.

Unfortunately, such denial does not block the effects of abuse. Instead, as we shall see, it makes the effects more harmful because the sources of the problems they create are unknown. Then the problems they create are more difficult to control and solve. Because of this all-too-prevalent process of denial, a sensitivity to the characteristics we are going to consider can help pastors identify survivors who are reticent or unable to identify themselves.

The purpose of this information is not merely to enable pastors to label persons as "abused." Although such an acknowledgment may be a healing step for a survivor, having such a label is not helpful. Survivors must come to that recognition on their own. A sensitive pastor may use his or her insights without ever saying, "I think you were abused." Such a pastor can provide the caring support so needed by survivors and can guide persons to helpful programs without ever saying, "You should participate in this because you were abused." These programs may not even be ones specifically designated for persons who were abused. They may be programs for the general population, but with a focus especially meaningful for persons from abusive backgrounds. We will discuss what such programs might be and how parishes can help establish them in chapter 8.

Recognizing the problems and behavior patterns of survivors can also help pastors be more patient with their behaviors. Such persons can do things that are confusing, frustrating, and even infuriating. If the sources of these behaviors are not understood, they can truly drive a pastor wild. But, I am ahead of myself. That is the subject of chapter 4.

The focus of this chapter is the recurring behavior patterns of grown-up abused children and the problems those patterns create. I will examine seven characteristics that are common to all grown-up abused children—lack of trust, low self-esteem, poor social skills, feelings of helplessness and powerlessness, inability to make decisions, inability to identify and express emotions, and phobias and flashbacks—and conclude with a discussion of the sexual problems of sex abuse survivors.

Lack of Trust

Trust is a basic element in all human relationships. On trust depends the ability to make friends, to form intimate relationships, and ultimately to establish lasting and fulfilling marriages. The ability to trust can be nurtured and strengthened by reflection, discussion, and structured experiences. But our fundamental orientation toward trust is formed by our basic life experiences. We learn to trust by having persons close to us treat us with respect, kindness, and consistency. We learn to trust by experiencing trustworthiness in others.

Erik Erikson (1963:247–251) maintains that the developmental process that disposes a person toward trust or mistrust is the first psychosocial crisis in human experience. It occurs primarily between birth and the age of two. Much of it happens literally at our mother's knee.

But what happens when that mother is abusive? What happens when that mother is inconsistent? What does a little boy learn when one day when he is hungry, he cries and he is fed, and yet the next day, when the same pain arises in his stomach and he initiates the same crying response, that same mother beats him and no food is forthcoming? What will the "bones remember" when one day a little girl approaches her mother with open arms and is picked up, cuddled, and caressed but the next day she is beaten and thrown across the room, and yet there is no apparent difference in the circumstances? This all too frequently is the experience of abused children. Twenty percent of reported abuse cases involve children under the age of two. The lessons learned are all too clear, "I can't trust my mother. Since I can't trust my mother, who can I trust?"

The child also learns another lesson. While this erratic process is going on, the child is trying to figure out, "What do I do to get a positive response? What will prompt my mother to give me food? What do I do to make sure she doesn't hit me?" The answer is, "I do not know. Nothing seems to work consistently. I must be doing something different from one time to another, but I can't figure out what it is. There must be something wrong with my instincts. I can't trust myself." The child has learned, "I cannot trust other people, and I cannot trust myself. They are untrustworthy and I am unreliable." All this is learned without the word "trust" ever being uttered.

Not all abuse starts in infancy. Initially parents may be caring and consistent, but later in childhood the relationship changes and becomes abusive. The reasons for this change can vary widely and are not the subject of this book. When the abusive and inconsistent behavior begins in later life, it is experienced at a more conscious level. Such experiences are more open to conscious reflection and redefinition than those remembered only "in the bones." However, the internal conflict is still the same. "If I can't trust my parents, who are supposed to love me, who can I trust? If I can't do anything right, I must be a worthless child."

The later-in-life experiences necessary to develop trust at this basic level for grown-up abused children must be comprehensive. They require frequent, constant, and consistent caring behavior in the face of regular disbelief and testing by the survivor. This can be a demanding process, as we shall see in chapter 4.

Low Self-esteem

The fact that abused children learn they cannot trust their parents creates other problems. As Erikson points out (1963:249), the ability to trust oneself and others "forms the basis in the child for a sense of identity which will later combine a sense of being 'all right,' of being oneself, and of becoming what other people trust one will become." The ability to trust and to feel trustworthy has a profound effect on children's perceptions of themselves. If their parents did not care enough about them to provide consistent love and care, the message that is internalized is that something is wrong with them. They are unlovable.

If learning you cannot trust your mother creates problems, what happens when you realize that your mother also did not love you? If your mother did not love you, who will? This devastating question and its natural conclusions confront every grown-up abused child. "My parents did not love me. I must have been an awful child. Sure, sometimes they said they loved me, but they acted otherwise. I must be a terrible person."

Such conclusions are natural for a grown-up abused child. This boy was not simply punished when he broke a toy or teased his sister or hung around with the wrong crowd. This girl was not simply reprimanded when she did poorly in school or stayed out too late. He was also ridiculed when he did well in school and was accused of being arrogant when he brought awards home. She was slapped around for no apparent reason and was told repeatedly that she was stupid, ugly, unlovable, and a slut. For these children the only consistent pattern in their life was abuse. There was no consistency to the reasons for which they were being punished.

In many cases these children were not only punished for the mistakes they made or the rules they broke, they were also punished for who they were. Their parents did not distinguish between their childhood clumsiness and adolescent misdeeds and the children themselves. The children were perceived as inherently evil, not merely as children who had done things that were wrong.

This failure to distinguish between the person and the deed was often coupled with the parents' unrealistic expectations. As pointed out in the discussion of neglect, many abused children are expected to fulfill roles in their families that are far beyond those appropriate to their age. This is not merely a result of the parents' own inadequacies and inabilities with their own parental roles. It can also be the result of unrealistic expectations and confusion over roles in the family.

Parents often expect their children to meet the parents' physical and emotional needs. Such children are expected not only to clean their own rooms but also the whole house. In addition, they are expected to be the parents' source of emotional support and the responsible decision-maker in the family. A child who fails in any of these adult tasks is branded as useless, bad, or even evil.

Years of being told that one is worthless and unlovable by the very person one expects to be the most understanding and accepting eventually takes its toll on one's self-image. Years of childhood inability to fulfill adult responsibilities, which one is made to believe one should assume, are convincing proof that one is worthless.

If anyone outside of the family treats the child as someone worthwhile, that person must be wrong or simply unaware of how bad the child really is. "He doesn't know what my mother knows about me." "If she knew me as well as my father does, she would not think so highly of me." The negative message has been well learned.

Poor Social Skills

If one does not trust oneself or other people, if one does not believe oneself to be worthwhile, one is not going to reach out to others. There is nothing to be gained. Friendship is practically unknown. The survivor is convinced that, even though people may be nice in the beginning, "They will soon turn against me. No one wants to be my friend anyway, because I have nothing to offer."

This approach to dealing with other people is a natural consequence of an abusive background. Such an attitude works against the possibility that an abused child will learn social skills. A person who is afraid to interact with other people, or is convinced that little or nothing can come from it, is not going to make much effort to make friends or gain any of the social experiences associated with doing so.

This hesitancy to initiate social contacts with others creates a vicious cycle. An abused child who finds it difficult to talk to others doesn't know where to start when it comes to forming friendships. Fear makes the child appear aloof and standoffish, so others are reluctant to take the initiative. This lack of response on the part of others confirms the abused child's sense of worthlessness and makes taking the first steps toward friendship more difficult. As a result, the child has few friends.

This lack of friends is perceived as another failure, another indication of worthlessness. The abused child does not have friends "because I am an uninteresting person." No one talks to the child "because I am not worth talking to." The child is convinced that "I am better off keeping to myself."

If someone does attempt to make friends with a grown-up who was an abused child, does try to get past the walls of aloofness and the barriers of isolation that have been erected in self-defense, that caring person may experience a wide variety of reactions from the survivor.

A prospective friend may experience distrust and even hostility because the survivor of abuse is sure that such caring behavior is not real and will not continue. Such suspicious responses are not the stuff of which strong friendships are made. Even the most caring and committed prospective friend will find his or her determination strained.

Another response that may be encountered is a grasping enthusiasm or suffocating attachment as the survivor seeks to fulfill a lifetime of needs for affection in a single relationship, trying to gain all the acceptance that was never found in the family. Such smothering attachment is also not the stuff on which friendships thrive. In either case, survivors exhibit poor social skills, which work against creating wholesome opportunities for such skills to be developed.

This problem of poor social skills is not merely the result of a survivor's lack of trust or feelings of poor self-worth. The family also failed to provide the normal opportunities that most children have to learn the basic social skills of conversation and discussion. A common trait of the abusive family is a lack of social interaction between its members. Typically, there is little or no general conversation and even less sharing of feelings and emotions. In fact, the latter are strongly discouraged and are often the occasion for violence. Such responses to discussion and sharing do not provide many occasions for developing the common social skills of conversation and communicating emotions.

Furthermore, children in abusive families are often hesitant to make friends with schoolmates. If the children are able to disguise the "faults" which are so evident to their parents, they may make friends with other children. But they must be careful not to become such good friends with their schoolmates that they will be expected to exchange reciprocal visits with one another. Such visits could have terrible consequences—their friends might find out how their parents treat them and learn what worthless persons they really are. It is safer to limit contacts with school-mates than to take the chance that others will really "find out" about them. Thus the learning of basic social skills that might occur through interactions outside the home is also limited because the abused children are afraid to allow them to develop.

Another consequence of this hesitancy to develop friendships is that the abused children never experience other families up close. They never learn that there are ways to relate to people, to confront disagreements, and to resolve conflicts that do not involve yelling, screaming, and fighting. They never learn to express their needs, to share confidences, and to rely on friends for assistance. When a group member was once chided for not sharing some of her fears and asking for assistance, she responded sadly, "I didn't know I was allowed." Many survivors never learn that there can be people who care about them and will help them.

All of this increases the isolation experienced by survivors and intensifies the feelings of mistrust and unworthiness that so color their lives. When their lives and relationships are controlled by such forces, the basic human tasks associated with forming and maintaining relationships become difficult and even excruciatingly painful. This will become evident in the next three traits to be discussed.

Feelings of Helplessness and Powerlessness

Because children are unable to determine what prompts caring behavior from their parents instead of assaults, they are unable to develop a sense of control or power over their lives. All human beings become empowered to give direction and purpose to their lives by learning to control the forces around them. This learning process begins with realizing one can get milk or a dry diaper by crying. It expands into learning to state one's needs in words, to communicate one's desires, and even to express an opinion different from one's parents and have that opinion respected. This learning involves a process of trial and error in a supportive environment where successes are applauded and mistakes are learned from.

This process does not happen in abusive families because abusive parents are inconsistent in the treatment of their children. Identical behaviors on the part of children elicit reactions that range from caring to cruelty, from praise to punishment. Such inconsistent reactions cause confusion and bewilderment. The children rightly feel that they cannot have any effect over their lives. They have no control over their environment. They are powerless.

As children grow older they go through many stages of development. Erikson (1963:251–261) maintains that the critical psychosocial crises that occur after the development of trust focus on the development of autonomy, initiative, and industry. By resolving these crises children learn to take control over their lives, make decisions about their actions, and achieve a sense of accomplishment through their activities. Each stage requires that a child learn new behaviors, take risks, and determine what achieves a desired end and what does not. In the process children experience power and achieve a sense of control over their lives.

In an abusive family this process is short-circuited. Children's attempts at independent action are indiscriminately punished or praised. Their initiatives are at one time encouraged, at another mocked or attacked, and their efforts to express themselves and to achieve self-determination are undermined and ridiculed. Instead of being encouraged and empowered to control their lives and destinies, the children learn to feel doubtful about their abilities, inferior to any task, and guilty about their efforts. Because the responses of their parents do not follow a rational or consistent pattern, the children cannot determine the connections between their behaviors and the outcomes they experience. Instead of gaining a sense of power, the children learn helplessness. Therefore, the prospect of assuming control over one's life becomes a task fraught with negative recollections. The possibility of undertaking new responsibilities in one's job becomes excruciatingly painful, and the act of making a decision becomes terrifying.

Inability to Make Decisions

Few of us enjoy making decisions. We prefer to get what we want without having to make difficult choices. We would really rather cruise through life on a smooth freeway without tempting exits and challenging detours. It would be nice if there were no sources of anxiety. Unfortunately, life does not work that way. We do have to make decisions and decide between options that may be equally enticing. Life's a hassle, but it's all we've got.

For grown-up abused children, the challenge of decision-making poses more than inconvenience and a few anxious moments. It is a task filled with doubt and guilt and a perceived inability to perform any task correctly. In addition to the emotional strain survivors may experience, the fact is that they simply may not know how to make decisions. The reasons for this can be summed up in five negatives: no models, no training, no opportunity, no measures, and no hope.

The first of these negatives, no models, arises from the fact that their own parents did not know how to make decisions, analyze options, or weigh consequences. Little effective decision-making was done in their homes, so, as children, they had no opportunity to observe the process in action and learn from it. They had no decision-making models to follow.

Grown-up abused children also had no training. Generally, their parents ignored them and let them survive by their own devices. As children they received no guidance as they struggled through the progressively more difficult decisions involved in childhood, adolescence, and, finally, adulthood. What they did learn about decision-making they learned by trial and error.

Also many abused children had no opportunity to make decisions. Their parents did not allow it. They severely restricted the options available to the children, told them precisely what to do—and the children were expected to like it. Whether or not they liked having alternatives imposed on them, the children were denied a critical opportunity to learn how to make decisions for themselves.

Even when abused children were allowed to make decisions, they were not provided with any clear measure of their effectiveness. All too often they were ignored to the extent that no one would respond to what decisions they did make. It was as if no decision had been made at all. No one said whether they had done a good job or a bad one. If the decision did have some negative consequences, no one was available to help them understand why and learn how to make better decisions in the future. They were never given tools to evaluate what they had done.

Also, frequently their parents would change the rules in the middle of the process; they would change the criteria for evaluation. Children would be told to do one thing and then be punished because they did not do something else. They would be told that their parents did not care what they did and then be beaten for what they did do. They would be encouraged to choose whatever they wanted and then would be punished if the choice did not coincide with what was secretly desired by their parents. They were never given clear criteria by which to judge whether they had done a good job.

And, finally, they had no hope. Besides never receiving guidance to help them make successful decisions, often the matters about which they were to decide were far beyond the level of maturity they had attained. They were forced to make decisions that should have been the responsibility of the adult members of the family. Too many variables were involved for them to expect to make the correct decision. They were thrown into situations in which they were almost guaranteed to fail. The end result of all these negatives is that adult abused children did not learn the correct process for decision-making, and the task itself became fraught with memories of failure and pain.

Grown-up abused children handle the anxiety related to decision-making in two different ways. One is simply to do nothing. They wait until circumstances make the decision for them. Someone has said, "Not to decide is to decide." The quote is frequently used as a challenge to those who fail to take stands on important issues. For survivors, the saying can be a source of consolation. It tells them that, if they wait long enough, the decision will be made for them and they will be relieved of the task and the anxiety attached to it.

The other way adult abused children manage the anxiety related to decision-making is to rush into a decision, to grab the first option available and run with it. When one acts this way one does not have to analyze alternatives and anguish over possible consequences. "Whatever decision I make will be wrong anyway, so why bother thinking about it?"

Neither method for decision-making is a very effective way to manage one's life. The first results in missed opportunities and a lack of control over one's life. I see this frequently in students who wait so long to choose their classes that they are closed out of the ones they want or need. Then they become depressed because "nothing ever works out for me."

The second response results in poorly conceived life choices. Such people seem to make the same mistake over and over again. This is often seen in the marriage patterns of survivors. They repeatedly make poor choices in lovers and mates. They attach themselves to anyone who responds positively without analyzing other aspects of the person's personality. They frequently end up in relationships that are harmful and even abusive, but they cannot understand what went wrong and why they made such a disastrous choice again.

Inability to Identify and Express Emotions

As I write about abuse, and I suspect that as you read about it, feelings well up. Major emotions for me are anger at what has happened to so many children and what difficult lives they have had. I ask you now to try to imagine what your feelings might be if you had been one of those abused children. Now tell yourself that you are not allowed to have such feelings. They are wrong and they are dangerous. Any sign of such feelings may result in more abuse.

Such is the dilemma of abused children. They have feelings but are forced to suppress them. They are not allowed to demonstrate their feelings and may be severely punished if they do.

Children who experience frequent and harsh violence in their families quite naturally feel anger at their attacker. Frequently the attacker is a parent. Anger at one's parents is wrong, says society: "Honor thy father and thy mother." So also says the parent, often with a few well-placed blows to reinforce the point.

Abused children also know that anger is a dangerous emotion. They have often experienced its damaging results. If, perchance, they expressed the anger they felt, they often received violence in return. In their experience, anger and violence are integrally connected; one automatically leads to the other. Seldom, if ever, have they seen someone be angry without some form of violence resulting. They do not want to be violent to others—they know how painful that can be. For them, to avoid violence one must avoid anger.

Therefore, many survivors learn to deny their feelings of anger. Even to acknowledge such feelings is too dangerous; it opens up too many negative possibilities. They will certainly feel guilty, they may be punished, and they may do something harmful to someone else.

Many group members insist adamantly that they do not and never have felt angry. They say this even as they grit their teeth and clench their fists. Their experiences have taught them that this feeling is something they should avoid at all costs. In order to avoid it they must deny its existence.

Other grown-up abused children may be able to admit their anger but not toward their parents. That is too wrong; that is too guilt provoking. So instead they express their anger toward other persons and things. One woman began to recall her abusive background as she shouted angry slogans during a rally against the Vietnam War. She suddenly realized that much of the vehemence behind her angry chants was really meant for her abusive parents.

Still other survivors report that they have acted in angry and even violent ways but they experienced no emotion at the time. They were in situations that rightly provoked anger and they acted accordingly, but did so with complete dispassion. Some reported that they felt as if they were standing outside of themselves, watching another person perform acts they recognized as angry and violent. The prospect of being angry was too threatening for them to allow themselves to be directly involved. They had to separate themselves from the person who was acting this way.

Much of such disassociation is because of the guilt that survivors experience over their feelings. Not only are they not supposed to be angry with their parents, but, because they are such worthless people, they have no right to be angry. It is thus doubly wrong to be angry at their parents.

This guilt associated with what most of us would consider justifiable anger creates other problems. Survivors believe that because their anger is wrong they deserve to be punished. Any time they have even the slightest sensation of anger they ought to be reprimanded. Because no one is available or willing to do so, they must do it themselves. Many grown-up abused children report acts of self-mutilation or suicide attempts following episodes of feeling angry toward their parents. They feel obliged to hurt themselves as a form of punishment or as a way to make up for what they have felt.

The problem of identifying and expressing feelings is associated not only with "negative" feelings of anger and guilt but also with positive emotions such as joy and satisfaction. Often adult abused children were punished for their childhood exuberance.

When they became excited and boisterous because something pleased them, they were slapped and told to shut up. When, as older children, they expressed satisfaction at their accomplishments, they were ridiculed and beaten for being proud and arrogant. One woman reported that the worst beating of her life occurred after she rushed home from school to show off the new uniform she had received when she made the school band. Her father beat her so violently she had to run out of the house to save herself.

Even normal responses to human situations were not acceptable. One group member told of a beating he received because his father found him crying over the death of his dog. "I'll give you something to really cry about" was the statement that preceded the beating.

The lessons learned from such experiences are that joy is dangerous and that pride and self-satisfaction is wrong. In short, all emotions should be suppressed; they certainly should not be expressed.

For most survivors, one emotion is constant and easily identifiable—fear. Most adult abused children continue to live in constant fear of being rejected and of being punished for anything and everything. They assess even the most minute actions for their potential for punishment, always expecting the worst. They are compulsive in their desire to please, always trying to determine what the people around them want, trying to anticipate their every desire. They must determine this so they will not be rejected. Thus, their emotional touchstone is anxiety as they attempt to identify and fill the emotional needs of others. At the same time, they ignore and deny their own needs and feelings. So much of their energy goes into dealing with the feelings of others, they never learn to recognize their own. Over and over again we have asked members of our groups to tell us what they are feeling, only to be met with blank stares. They do not even recognize the question as an appropriate one.

Flashbacks and Phobias

It should be evident from our discussion that grown-up abused children find it necessary to repress and deny many of their experiences. They are too painful; they are too disorienting for the children to allow them fully into their consciousness. If they allowed themselves to feel the pain and anguish being imposed upon them, they would be totally overwhelmed. Therefore, they continually try to push them from their memories.

William Sloane Coffin (1981) once graphically pointed out that the digestive system of the human psyche does not have an elimination canal. "What goes down must come up." This astute observation is the nemesis of adult abused children. As much as they want to forget, as effectively as they may have blocked their experiences in order to survive, memories of these experiences all too frequently pop back up at unusual, unexpected, and embarrassing times. Often such recollections come unannounced and without warning. Frequently they seem to lack any association with reality. The memories that suddenly appear are not about anything of which they have any previous recollection. They have images of being physically beaten or sexually abused—incidents of which they have no conscious memory.

Such unexpected memories often offer clues to specific forms of abuse or particularly violent episodes of abuse for persons who are already aware that they were abused. Many people remember experiences of physical abuse but have no recollection of sexual abuse. After time in a Grown-Up Abused Children group, some survivors begin to recall and reexperience the incidents of sexual abuse.

Such memories and flashbacks can also be the key to understanding early forms of abuse, those which happened almost before the child could cognitively define them. Such sensory images are reports about what "the bones remember." As painful as these recollections are, they are signs of health. The survivors begin to have such memories when they are strong enough to deal with the realities of their past. Their psyche can finally allow them to remember without being totally overwhelmed—as overwhelming as such experiences may seem at first. They will need help to integrate this new information, but they are taking an important step toward putting their lives back together.

Another way that past abusive experiences are regurgitated from the psychological digestive system is through strange and unexplained phobias. One woman returned to the group after the holidays. She had spent Christmas Day with friends. As they were seated at dinner, she became so anxious that she had to leave the table. She said, "I don't know what caused this, but I am sure it has some relationship to my abuse." As we discussed the incident, we also discussed the dining patterns of her family. She soon realized that she always sat to the left of her father at dinner and he frequently hit her viciously, knocking her out of her chair. At the Christmas dinner she had been seated to the left of another male guest. The similarity to her family situation was subconsciously so threatening she had to leave. She ended the discussion by saying, "Now that I know why I felt so anxious, I think I could control it in the future. Before, I didn't know what was going on in me, so I couldn't make myself distinguish the present from the past."

It is important for survivors to pay close attention to these phobias and flashbacks. They must not write them off as hallucinations or other examples of the craziness so often attributed to them by their parents. They must examine them as important sources of information about the past and the ways in which it influences their present.

There is a strong similarity between such experiences for adult abused children and a phenomenon that has received much notoriety because of the experiences of Vietnam veterans. Many veterans have reported experiences of flashbacks, of unexplained recollections and reexperiencing of battle situations long after they returned home. The disorienting aspects of reliving such traumatic events has become known as post-traumatic stress disorder. It is a widely accepted psychological diagnosis. It is easy to see that survivors of abuse would be susceptible to post-traumatic stress disorder. In fact, the frequent and sustained violence experienced by defenseless children may well be the ultimate in trauma. We will examine this phenomenon in greater detail in chapter 9.

Sexual Problems

Based on what we have said so far, it does not require great psychological sophistication to deduce that sexual abuse creates sexual problems. All abuse attacks a person's bodily integrity. However, sexual abuse constitutes a violation of a person in the most private and intimate way. It is also the most profound violation of a person's trust, because sexual abuse, as we are considering it, constitutes sexual activity between a trusted family member or friend and a nonconsenting child. It thus destroys not only the child's bodily integrity but also her (or his) confidence in previously trusting relationships.

Sexual abuse is probably the most devastating form of abuse because of the intimate nature of the violation and the secrecy and privacy involved. Sex is a private, intimate, even secret activity. When such acts are performed outside the "normal" parameters for such activity, the level of secrecy increases. In sexual abuse, the secrecy imposed reaches its zenith. To the natural privacy associated with sexual activity is added another message of secrecy and shame.

The perpetrator carefully constructs opportunities to be alone with the victim. He communicates to the victim the secrecy of the act. Sometimes this is done in cajoling manner: "This is just between you and me." "We won't be able to go to the park again if you tell Mother what we have done." At other times the message is imprinted in the mind of the victim by threats and beatings. "If you tell anyone, I will hurt your mother."

The sexual abuse victim is often aware that other members of the family are participants in the secrecy. Mother quietly ignores the abuse or makes vicious or disparaging remarks about "Daddy's little girl," all the while offering no help or assistance. This enforces the need for secrecy and the associated sense of guilt and shame.

Even when the sexual abuse is truly a secret in the family, the survivor usually believes this is because people choose to ignore anything related to the sexual activity. Because it is too shameful to be considered, they prefer to look the other way. This reinforces the sense of shame and the need for silence.

Furthermore, when sexual abuse does become public, the people who become involved respond with great horror and dismay. Often the authorities become involved and the family is broken up. Although such procedures are intended to protect the child, they are emotionally disruptive and often create further feelings of shame and guilt for the victim, who is revictimized by the very processes set up as protection. Such consequences seem to be the unavoidable result of the evil actions in an imperfect world which has not yet devised effective ways to heal the effects of evil.

Karen Leaman (1980:22) has pointed out how important it is for parents to react with care and concern toward children who may have experienced sexual abuse. They should be careful not to overreact in horror and dismay; such reactions simply intensify the child's sense of shame and guilt. This is difficult for all parents and impossible for many. The horror they feel is simply overwhelming. Sometimes parents are the people least able to provide the support a child needs. This is an area where sensitive and caring pastors can have a significant impact on the future mental and spiritual health of child victims.

When children are sexually abused, they can learn two very different things. One thing they sometimes learn is that sex—and any form of intimate physical contact—is wrong, ugly, and threatening. For such survivors (and women are the most frequent victims), any form of intimate contact with a man creates tremendous anxiety. Even a friendly hug in passing can stir painful memories or precipitate great fear. The hug is perceived as a prelude to forced sexual intercourse. For such women even the ritual hugs at our group sessions are threatening, but because they are performed in a safe and public environment they can produce meaningful learnings. As these women experience caring contact without further sexual intimacy, they learn that such contacts can be separated from sexual activity and need not be occasions of great fear.

Those women who are able to establish loving and intimate relationships with a man are nevertheless frequently afflicted with recollections of abusive sexual episodes. Many report flashbacks of abusive experiences in the midst of lovemaking. Such experiences place a cloud of apprehension over all future acts of intimacy and constitute a great deterrent to fulfilling sexual relations within marriage.

Some survivors of sexual abuse find the mere thought of sex with a man so frightening or distasteful that they opt for a lesbian relationship. Sexual abuse experiences do not explain all homosexual preferences and may not even be the sole reason for persons who experienced abuse. However, it is easily understandable that some women are too frightened by their past experiences to even consider the heterosexual alternative.

Women who were sexually abused as children may also learn a quite different behavior. They may learn to be flirtatious and even promiscuous in their relationships with men. These women have learned that the primary way to gain acceptance, approval, and affection from men is to offer themselves as eager sex partners. Such sexual relations may or may not be satisfying, but that is not the issue. The purpose is not to establish a satisfying relationship but to gain acceptance by whatever method works.

To date, little research has been done on boys who experienced sexual abuse. Although the incidents may in fact be less frequent than those of abuse of girls, there is increasing evidence that it happens more frequently than previously believed. The abuse may be either of a homosexual or heterosexual nature. If the sexual abuse is mother to son, there is evidence that the response will be similar to those described above for women who were abused by males: that is, aversion or excessive acting out. In the latter case the men are often trying to reassert their manhood.

If the abuse is father to son, multiple confusions are created. The grown-up abused child may experience an aversion to the behavior of the abusive father but have severe questions about his sexual identity and manhood. He may also question his ability to perform in a heterosexual manner. The young man clearly lacks models for normal sexual activity. When stricken with the typical confusion of puberty, such survivors are practically guaranteed more than their fair quotient of adolescent anxieties.

Whatever the manner of response exhibited, survivors of sexual abuse experience a high level of confusion about their sexual identity and about appropriate methods of sexual expression. This creates numerous problems for them as they seek to develop intimacy, establish loving relationships, and even select a mate with whom they might have a satisfying sexual relationship.

These questions are, of course, critical for all people. Every pastor knows that these important life choices affect everyone's prospects for happiness. It is therefore important that pastors become increasingly conscious of the dynamics involved in this and all forms of abuse. Such information can help pastors more effectively care for and heal those whose lives are so severely disrupted by sexual abuse.

Such information is needed to understand the effects of all forms of abuse better, effects that extend beyond the immediate burns and bruises and belittling. These immediate acts of abuse, as harmful as they are, impart lessons that diminish the whole life of survivors. They convey negative messages to the persons who experienced the abuse, messages that last a lifetime. These messages also tell survivors how to relate to other people. Such methods may have been necessary and appropriate in an abusive family, but they are counterproductive in a nonabusive environment. However, survivors were never taught how to distinguish one situation from the other, and so they misapply the skills they learned so well.

4

Behaviors
That Try the Patience
of a Saint

To say that the behaviors of survivors can be so dysfunctional as to tempt even the most patient person to be angry and rejecting is not to blame the victim. Rather, it is a warning to persons who must deal with survivors that the actions of adults who were abused as children can be extremely aggravating. Understanding and patience are critical.

Neither can one argue that the behavior of abused children causes the violence they receive. No childhood mischief justifies the violence that is reported by child protective agencies. It is true that abused children are often rebellious, disobedient, and disruptive. Many teachers report that children from abusive homes exhibit severe discipline problems. The question is whether their rebellious behavior is the reason they were abused or whether it is the result of their abuse. Is their behavior something they have learned at home or is it their way of acting out feelings generated at home which they dare not act upon there?

Certainly, the disruptive actions of children in school must be corrected and controlled. So also must the inappropriate and sometimes violent actions of adults be modified and corrected. However, one's approach to that correction will differ greatly depending on whether the actions are considered the result of inherent evil or the result of destructive forces imposed upon these children by their families.

The patience required is more easily found if we understand the reasons for the behavior with which we are dealing. Armed with such information, we will have better insight as to how to modify the behavior, which will help the survivor achieve a desired relationship with other people. If we can understand the source of the problem, maybe we can help survivors change dysfunctional behaviors to ones that will be productive.

A few years ago an informal discussion at a clergy gathering turned to my work with grown-up abused children. The discussion continued for some time as pastors continued to probe me with questions about the actions of grown-up abused children. I was surprised by the intensity of their interest. When the group broke for dinner, one pastor identified the reason for his enthusiasm for the topic. "You have just helped me understand a number of parishioners who have been driving me crazy," he said. "I knew they came from abusive backgrounds, but I did not understand what bearing that had on their present behavior." The purpose of this chapter is to share some of the content of that discussion and to highlight some of the behaviors common to survivors that are not only dysfunctional for them but aggravating for those who must live and work with them as their pastors, teachers, fellow workers, or spouses. Not all these behaviors are unique to survivors of abuse, but they are often more intense and pervasive in such persons. If we see such behaviors, it may be helpful to ask if they are the result of abusive backgrounds. If that is the cause, certain responses will make these persons easier to deal with and will be helpful to the survivors themselves.

Attachment to Approval

We have seen that grown-up abused children do not think very highly of themselves. They consider themselves worthless and unlovable. This is the message they have learned and internalized from their families. When they encounter someone who says something different, who affirms them as a person and accepts them as someone of value, their reaction may be one of two very different kinds: They may be pleasantly surprised and enthralled with such approval, or they may be suspicious and become anxious because the experience is so unfamiliar to them.

The person who is able to accept the positive messages may find the experience so exhilarating that he or she becomes strongly attached to the source of that approval: Finally, here is someone or some group that accepts and appreciates the survivor as an individual of value.

Because pastors and religious congregations at least attempt to be accepting and caring of the people with whom they come in contact, they may become beacons to those who have suffered abuse. The light of unconditional acceptance may lure survivors the way a light attracts moths. A survivor of abuse may bask in the light of approval randomly and compulsively without understanding why the light is so attractive or how it can be used to best advantage. The survivor has found a place where he or she can receive approval and affirmation never received at home. In this hunger for affection the survivor may become compulsively attached to the pastor or other persons or groups within the congregation. The pastor or members of the congregation may, without understanding what is happening, become surrogate parents and families. Although such surrogate relationships can be beneficial, the parties involved need to understand the basis of the relationship. Otherwise, the extent and intensity of the attachment can become confusing and counterproductive.

Most pastors have experienced an excessive attachment on the part of a parishioner. Such relationships are time-consuming and overwhelming, and pastors may find it necessary to discourage the relationship and create distance between themselves and the parishioner. If this parishioner experienced child abuse, even the most cautious and tactful efforts to discourage the excessive attachment and create a more balanced and healthy relationship may be experienced by the adult abused child as another form of disapproval and rejection. Once again the parishioner feels unworthy of acceptance and affection.

This does not mean that pastors should not seek to define and clarify the proper nature of their relationship with a survivor. It is critical that such a person learn to develop appropriate and healthy relationships. The pastor who believes that a member of the congregation has or is experiencing some form of abuse must always be very careful to explain why there is not enough time to talk at this particular time or why it is impossible to arrange for a particular meeting. The pastor must assure the person that this lack of time does not imply lack of caring, and the pastor should then try to create other opportunities for acceptance and approval from persons or groups within the congregation. In this way the survivor can receive the necessary support without becoming a drain on the pastor's time.

The pastor who believes that the parishioner is a survivor may also find it appropriate to discuss this background with the parishioner and offer help in acknowledging the source of this strong need for acceptance and approval. The pastor can explain that there are many ways to gain acceptance and many people from whom to receive it. The pastor is not the only person from whom it is possible to receive love; there are, in fact, many other people who find the survivor attractive, appealing, and worthwhile. The pastor can help the parishioner understand that because someone is not always sufficiently responsive, this lack of response does not constitute rejection. Lack of responsiveness may be the result of a person's own lack of ability or because of other demands on his or her time. Of course, all this requires great delicacy, because survivors are highly sensitive to any hint of failure on their part, and the survivor who believes that lack of responsiveness is a result of something he or she did will assume that it is a sign of personal worthlessness and failure as a human being.

Truth Found in Testing

Another reaction of survivors to acceptance and approval is disbelief and distrust. Adult abused children may be attracted to persons or groups who say they are worthwhile and lovable, but they will still be suspicious and skeptical. To such people approval is gratifying but disconcerting. They are constantly wondering, "Is it real?" "Will it last?" They are sure there must be some mistake. They cannot be comfortable with what is happening or relax and bask in the glow of being loved. They live with the abiding fear that the approval will soon stop.

Some survivors describe receiving approval as having the first shoe drop. The second shoe falls when that approval is withdrawn and they are told again that they are worthless and useless. The one constant in their families was that approval was never consistent. It was always subject to being revoked, always open to being rescinded. When the anxiety of waiting for the second shoe becomes too much, some survivors feel compelled to make it fall. They begin to bait those who are giving them approval. Their expectation of rejection prompts them to examine every statement of approval for a hint of insincerity or inconsistency. They question and challenge any sign of approval. They will test and probe and scrutinize.

Such constant testing can become aggravating. One begins to feel that one is always being examined. No statement is ever taken at face value. Every question is asked three different ways to see if the same answer is forthcoming. Subjects one thought had been put to rest long ago are resurrected to see if the answer has been revised. In our support groups this meant that old issues frequently were brought up in new guises to see if the leaders' responses were the same. It also meant that whenever a member shared new personal information, the leaders were always asked, "Do you still like me?"

One of my co-leaders has kept in touch with a former group member for several years. She is still asked regularly, "Do you still like me?" If the slightest hint of annoyance creeps into the co-leader's response, the former group member hears it as a sign of rejection. Such constant testing can put a strain on a relationship and try the patience of a saint.

Pastors must be prepared for such testing. Survivors may be highly suspicious of the motivations of religious leaders. They assume that expressions of pastoral concern are merely programmed responses. They may take it as a personal challenge to prove that clergy are no different from all the other people who have rejected them in the past.

It is important that pastors maintain their equanimity but still point out, gently yet firmly, why such testing and challenges are not necessary. No shortcut exists for this process. Grown-up abused children have learned to distrust those closest to them through many years of brutally ingrained training. To learn a different lesson will also take time.

Manipulation as Survival

This constant questioning and testing is a form of manipulation. It is the survivor's way of controlling the relationship with the giver of approval. He or she is trying to determine what response or ways of acting will gain acceptance from people. Such manipulation is annoying and revolting to someone accustomed to honest and direct dealings. Most of us get angry when we feel we are being manipulated, that someone is trying to put something over on us, to get us to do something we do not really want to do. Manipulation may also mean someone is trying to get something fraudulently. We believe that when someone is manipulative they are trying to get something they don't deserve or get out of something they do deserve. Our response is to try to thwart such behavior.

As understandable as such a response is, it is not appropriate when dealing with survivors. They are not accustomed to dealing with people directly. Their family situation was so chaotic and the forms of communications so convoluted that they were required to assess and question the motives and intentions of their family members. Roles were not clearly defined. Expectations were never voiced. Requests were not made directly. Their parents seldom responded directly to the needs their children expressed. Therefore, if the children wanted anything they had to find indirect manipulative ways to attain them. They were forced to manipulate their parents in order to get approval and to have their basic needs for affection met. This was often true even of their most basic human needs.

For grown-up abused children, manipulation was the only way

they learned to get what they needed and still avoid being beaten and ridiculed. They had to cover up Mother's drinking so that Father would not beat her or them. They had to learn to say only what their fathers wanted to hear so they would be allowed to have dinner. They had to respond to their uncle's sexual requests so he would not fulfill his threats to harm them or their brothers and sisters. These grown-up abused children learned at a young age to know what people around them wanted and to respond quickly in order to avoid trouble and receive a modicum of approval. This was manipulation, but it was necessary for survival.

Such manipulative responses become almost robotlike. They are automatic and unconscious; the survivors are not even aware their actions are manipulative. A pastor working with a survivor must constantly remember that the manipulation is not malicious. One must constantly be in touch with one's feeling of being manipulated and remind oneself of the source and reason for such behavior. Moral judgments must be avoided.

But even as moral judgments are avoided, corrective action must be taken. Pastors must avoid being trapped into giving their own opinion on topics and must provide as much latitude as possible for differences of opinion. They can encourage survivors to disagree with them. They can create situations on committees and work projects where their own preferences are not known so the survivor is forced to express an opinion without any other opinion with which to link it. When such occasions arise the pastor can point out the value of having different opinions expressed, the variety of insights that can be gained through such a process, and the fact that people can disagree without becoming angry and abusive. If the survivor has acknowledged an abusive background, the pastor can take the opportunity to point out how such experiences are different from what used to happen in the family, help the survivor reflect on the new experiences, and then show how to apply the learning to other situations. In this way the survivor can learn that manipulation is no longer necessary for survival.

Safety in Sensitivity

In order to manipulate people one must be able to read their every move, recognize their every desire, and anticipate their every need before it is stated. These are skills that survivors learn quickly.

I discovered early in my work with grown-up abused children that they often read my moods faster than I recognized them myself. They were tuned in to my every facial expression and to every message communicated by my body. I often point out to prospective group leaders, all of whom are psychologists, counselors, or social workers, that they have paid big bucks to learn what these people learned as children—how to recognize the moods and emotional needs of others.

On one occasion, my co-leader confessed to me after a meeting that she had had a particularly bad day and was in a bad mood. She hoped it had not shown in the meeting. I assured her I had not noticed, so I was sure that the group members had not noticed either. At the beginning of the next meeting, I discovered how wrong I had been. All the members of the group had noticed and had compared notes between meetings. They wanted to know what had been wrong, because they needed to make sure it was not something they had done.

This incident was exceptional only because of the way the group handled it. They actually confronted my co-leader and tried to deal with the issues involved. More typically, they would have identified a problem and then sought to avoid it. In this instance, some of the group members met by chance during the week and compared their impressions. They realized they shared a common perception, and this gave them the courage to bring up the issue. Such a process is the exception rather than the rule.

Usually, instead of using their highly developed sensitivity to the moods and feelings of others as a means of establishing stronger and more intimate relationships, survivors use these skills as tools to avoid conflicts and potentially emotional situations. They recognize conflicts early and then work frantically to avoid them rather than resolve them.

This is a natural reaction, since they developed their skills in situations that frequently resulted in violence. They learned to recognize the moods and feelings of their parents or abusive spouses in order to protect themselves. It was essential that they determine quickly whether their father was in a good or a bad mood the moment he walked in the room, so they would know whether to run to greet him or run and hide, talk about what happened at school or quietly bury themselves in the corner with a book. Should the wife talk and joke with her husband or quickly and quietly put dinner on the table? Survivors learned quickly and well the telltale signs that indicate a person's mood—whether the shoulders are hunched or straight, the face relaxed or tense, the hands open or clenched. They learned to read all these signs instinctively and instantly. They learned to do it unconsciously, without thinking.

The defensive use of this sensitivity to the moods of others means that abuse survivors often do not form close friendships. Sometimes they are attracted to someone, but when they detect that the person is having a bad day they shy away, because they fear the bad mood may mean that the person will become violent toward them. They fear that their friend will turn on them and treat them like their parents did when they had a bad day.

The potential friend becomes confused and disenchanted. Why is the survivor suddenly so distant when they are together? The friend understandably becomes impatient with the erratic nature of the relationship and may decide to quit trying to make it work. The survivor has inadvertently destroyed a relationship by misapplying a skill that should have made the relationship more intimate. Because of deeply ingrained fears, this ability to be sensitive to the moods and needs of a friend has proven to be a liability rather than an asset.

The pastor who is aware that certain parishioners are abuse survivors can be aware of their tendency to be defensively sensitive to the moods of other people. The pastor can be very explicit about his about his or her own moods when dealing with them, being careful to explain what has caused a bad day, for example, and pointing out that it has nothing to do with them. He or she can also be aware when survivors are misapplying their sensitivity to other members of the congregation. In such instances, the pastor can intervene by helping to interpret to the survivor what is really happening. Such interventions demand patience, but they can be a great help to survivors as they strive to develop supportive relationships within a congregation. Both they and the congregation can grow from such a process.

Excessive Control

Abuse victims learn early that they have little control over their lives. When parents are inconsistent in their reactions, children cannot learn what actions to perform to achieve desired outcomes. Nor were survivors given many opportunities when they were young to make decisions. They were told what to do and severely punished when they did anything else. Therefore, they seek every possible way to limit the negative influences in their lives. Viewing every person or incident as potentially harmful, they seek to keep their relationships to a minimum, avoiding outside contacts as much as possible and limiting the possibilities of what might happen in relationships with others. In short, they strive for as much control as possible.

This can be frustrating to people with whom survivors may be dealing. Friends want to have more frequent contacts, to engage in new kinds of activities. Survivors, on the other hand, want to keep such things at a minimum so the possibilities for negative experiences can also be held to a minimum. New experiences are a threat to survivors. Since their assumption is that new experiences are going to be negative, it is safer to avoid them than to try anything new. It is better to make sure nothing new happens than to have something happen that could turn out to be unsafe. It is better to have a severely limited but safe environment than one filled with opportunities that may lead to disaster. Such limiting of experiences deters the freedom and spontaneity necessary for satisfying relationships with others.

This lack of spontaneity, this controlling approach to life, is not just related to external activities. It is also the pattern for survivors' approaches to their emotions. Many of them control their emotional expressions so completely that they are practically nonexistent. Their willingness and ability to share their feelings is severely limited. Once again, this is something they learned early in life; it was not safe to express emotions because they were met with abuse. This lack of emotional response is so common among very young abused children that social workers have given it a name: "frozen watchfulness." Social workers observed that many abused children were extremely restrained in their response to normally emotional situations. Such children would sit quietly for long periods without any visible response. However, the social workers observed that they were fully aware of what was happening around them and prepared to respond instantly in a defensive manner.

Such excessive control of emotions can also be very frustrating for persons trying to relate to a grown-up abused child. Survivors' discomfort with emotions and their inability to share feelings make it difficult for a prospective friend to get to know them and their needs and preferences. Friends are unable to determine what pleases them, excites them, encourages them, or distresses them. Thus, a survivor's friend must guess what he or she wants to do for an evening or what completely turns the person off. The grown-up abused child learned long ago that his or her preferences were not important; personal needs would not be met and, in fact, might often be directly contradicted. Therefore it was safer not to express needs, not to acknowledge preferences, not to ask for anything. After years of active denial, such survivors are no longer conscious of even having needs or wishes. When asked what they would like to do, how they feel about something, or what someone can do to help them, "I don't know" is an accurate description of their level of personal awareness.

As accurate as such a statement may be, it is still frustrating for the would-be friend trying to get to know such a person. It is still trying to the patience. This excessive control of personal expression contravenes all of a friend's desires and efforts to establish meaningful communication and sharing.

Pastors may encounter the effects of this tendency toward excessive control when they attempt to involve survivors in new activities in the parish. Special efforts must be made. Pastors may need to make individual contacts with such persons, pointing out the advantages of new opportunities even as they acknowledge the fears and anxieties the survivors may be feeling. Pastors may even have to accompany such persons to their first meeting. As time-consuming as this may be in the beginning, it can be the opportunity for new growth for the survivor and an occasion for the congregation to gain a new active member.

Comfort with Chaos

Even though survivors strive valiantly to control their emotions and achieve control over the circumstances of their lives, they nevertheless exhibit a great affinity for chaos. As has been pointed out, one of the few predictable factors in an abusive family is its inconsistency, its chaos. Little structure or order exists, family roles are frequently shifted, personal expectations and demands constantly change. Such confusion, as disruptive and destructive it may be, is the experience most familiar to grown-up abused children. It is the mode of operation with which they are familiar.

Therefore, these people lack the ability to concentrate for long on a single task or to complete an assignment. They do not understand the importance of bringing topics of conversation to satisfactory conclusions. They have no sense of how to plan the details of events and actions. They lack any notion of what it means to establish priorities and act accordingly; such processes are foreign to their experience. They do not understand how to focus their attention and plan for contingencies, and they do not even know why it is important to do so. What is all the fuss about? Isn't it better just to hang loose? Everything will work out—as well as anything ever does. Of course, this drives normally well-organized people absolutely bananas, but survivors do not understand why there is a problem.

Another dimension is that for many survivors experiencing a structured environment is not only difficult but frightening. For many adults abused as children, the only time attention in their families was focused was when violence was being directed at someone. The only time they knew someone was paying attention to them was when they were being yelled at or abused. The only time there was any evidence that people cared about them was when they got angry. For these people, the experience of having someone's undivided attention was a threatening and painful experience and meant they were going to be hit or ridiculed.

For such persons a chaotic, nonfocused environment is safer, because it means that no one, especially themselves, is being abused. Such people are actually more comfortable with chaos, because they feel the likelihood of violence is lessened when many things are happening at the same time. If there is little plan or forethought to events, if there is no schedule that anyone is expected to follow, there is less possibility that anyone will become upset, that anyone can be blamed if things "don't turn out."

This may have been an effective way to avoid violence in their families, but it exasperates anyone who is not operating from such a background or from such premises. Other people cannot understand why survivors do not plan for events, get nervous when someone suggests that they plan, do not follow plans that are made, and seem to undermine all efforts at rational organization.

Of course, such a propensity for chaos can be extremely disconcerting for a pastor who is trying to work with members of the congregation in task-oriented committees or who is trying to get church members to share with one another about their lives and spiritual growth. To incorporate survivors effectively into such groups, the pastor must have finely tuned group process skills and be able gently yet firmly to cut off extraneous comments and keep the group on target.

I used to be a very laid-back group leader. I believed that with minimal guidance and a few well-placed questions a group could develop its own leadership and maintain its commitment to the task. When I started working with grown-up abused children, I quickly learned that such an approach was not going to work with these groups. I became a tyrant—at least by my previous standards. I developed a format for the groups and stuck to it firmly. I became quick to point out comments that were off the topic and to control persons who rambled on at length. Occasionally, there was resistance to such restrictions, but usually the group members came to appreciate the structure that had been imposed. Although they did not use this language, they found the structure itself therapeutic.

Pastors may find it necessary to employ the same tactics when working with survivors within their congregations. They may encounter some resistance, but generally the survivors will appreciate and learn from the experience. Parishioners who are not survivors will feel considerably less frustration. If a pastor has an open relationship with a survivor about former abuse, he can discuss disruptive behaviors and help in understanding their origins. The survivor can be more conscious about trying to change and can become aware that such avoidance behaviors are not necessary in nonabusive environments.

Inappropriate Reactions

The subjects discussed in this chapter are all examples of inappropriate and potentially disruptive reactions to normal life experiences. Such reactions are dysfunctional and counterproductive. The list is not exhaustive. I would like to end this chapter by identifying a few of the less complicated but equally confusing and annoying reactions.

Persons who have in the past or even now experience violence in their families may have many different situations to which they have negative or even frightening reactions. These situations may trigger anxiety toward something that would not normally be considered threatening. They may trigger hostile responses to situations or to the comments of others that would normally be considered innocuous, inoffensive, or even encouraging.

Some examples in earlier chapters have referred to the kinds of reactions survivors may have to situations that consciously or subconsciously remind them of circumstances from their past, such as the woman who had to leave a holiday dinner table because she was seated to a man's left. I have also discussed the problems survivors have with touching or being touched. Whether it is a gentle pat on the back or a friendly hug, physical contact strikes terror in their hearts and they react with startled withdrawal or freeze with fear. In some cases they experience physical nausea. Such responses confuse those who observe them and may lead others to brand the survivor as "strange." It may also convince a prospective friend that the survivor does not want to be friendly. Of course, such is not the case, but the adult abused child's reaction has communicated that message.

Another example of an inappropriate reaction occurred in a Grown-up Abused Children group. A male member was so soft-spoken that group members often would ask him to speak louder. Invariably he would become angry and refuse to talk at all after such encouragement. This happened several times before we were able to get him to explain the reasons for his anger, but after much pressure he finally blurted it out. "You people are just like my father. You are always making fun of the way I talk."

The explanation for his outburst was that he had not learned to talk until he was almost four years old. His family members, especially his father, ridiculed him for this, and his speech became a continuing subject of family derision. As a result, he became very sensitive to any comments about his speech; even comments intended to encourage him to express his ideas were interpreted as negative and demeaning. Only after extensive discussion in the group was he able to understand the difference between positive comments about his speech and those intended to ridicule.

Another example is a woman who reported feeling extremely anxious whenever she saw a tank of fish. One day, while visiting a pet shop with a friend who was purchasing tropical fish for her son, her anxiety became so overwhelming she almost fainted. Fortunately, her friend recognized something was wrong, got her out of the pet store, and found a place where they could talk. As they discussed her anxiety, she became aware of her first recollections of these aquariums. Her father had had several in his den. Then she recalled that her father had sexually abused her as a small child and that his fish were the only thing she had had to look at while he was attacking her. She had completely blocked the sexual abuse and had transferred her anxiety to the aquariums.

Once she made the connection, she not only began to enjoy tropical fish but, more importantly, was able to deal constructively with the effects of the sexual abuse as they affected her relationships with others, especially men.

As these few examples indicate, the situations to which survivors can have inappropriate reactions are extremely diverse and difficult to predict. Adverse reactions can arise to the most ordinary objects and in the most innocuous situations. It is difficult for most of us to understand these connections between past circumstances and present events. The experiences of survivors are often so bizarre and different from our own experience that we find them difficult to comprehend, even when they are explained.

However, when parishioners have unusual reactions to normal events and situations, pastors should consider them worth investigating, especially if the parishioner is known to be a survivor of abuse. All of us have experiences from our past that color the way we perceive the present. Fortunately, most of those effects are positive. They provide us with insights and skills that help us understand, analyze, and respond creatively to present events.

Survivors have had negative experiences with situations that are normally positive, experiences that gave them false information and maladaptive skills. These experiences may have been so brutal that the details have been blocked from conscious memory; all that remains is a reaction to specific stimuli. These stimuli (such as an aquarium) re-create the anxiety, pain, and defense reactions associated with the original event, without recalling the event itself.

Many survivors have large blocks of their lives for which they have no memories and images of violence and pain for which they have no explanation. Such experiences, coupled with bizarre reactions to commonplace objects and events, are the result of severe trauma. They are symptoms of post-traumatic stress disorder, mentioned briefly in chapter 3. Simply put (we will discuss this at greater length in chapter 9), persons experiencing extreme stress block many of their physical reactions and emotional feelings in order to survive, either physically or emotionally. Having blocked these events from their conscious memory, some parts of the experience may reappear at seemingly unconnected and irrational moments. Just as the blocking was part of the defense process, recollections and images are part of the healing process. They are part of the psyche's effort to reintegrate the traumatic event in their lives.

Because such experiences occur, pastors should not dismiss the irrational and inappropriate reactions of abuse survivors or view their accounts of unexplainable images and visions of violence as products of strange or sick minds. Such occurrences may be the mark of a strong personality that has survived extreme trauma and is now striving to regain its full health. Taking these accounts seriously and working closely with parishioners to help them understand their admittedly bizarre behavior will reassure them that they are not losing their minds, or hallucinating, and help them regain their memories and reintegrate the parts of their lives they have lost.

It is amazing to observe how clarifications about single small events in a survivor's life can result in significant changes in the way he or she responds to situations and relates to people. Such insights can improve a survivor's effectiveness, productivity, and happiness: no small accomplishment!

It is impossible to identify all the circumstances to which survivors may have irrational reactions or exhibit inappropriate behaviors. Their lives, as are the lives of all of us, are so diverse and complex that the possibilities are infinite. The examples and the explanations in this chapter are provided to enable religious leaders to be more understanding and sensitive to the needs of survivors. This knowledge will help in recognizing the reasons for these behaviors, in supporting survivors in their struggle, and in giving them the skills necessary to develop new, healthier responses to the world around them. Then survivors too can experience the joy of a God who is "not a God of confusion but of peace" (1 Cor. 14:33).

5

Family Values
and Family Violence

An important part of a pastor's ability to deal effectively with both victims and survivors of abuse is theological orientation. Beliefs regarding the family—the role of parents, children, and spouses and what is expected of each—can have profound effects on the pastor's ability to respond with understanding and sensitivity.

A powerful presumption exists that religious institutions are committed to family values. Churches and synagogues have a justifiably positive reputation in this area. However, too often they hold a narrow theological definition of marriage and what should be involved in preserving it. This restricted definition creates problems in the ways the church exhibits its commitment and in the advice given by its spokespersons. The focus of this commitment and advice is primarily on keeping couples together, preserving the institution of marriage—for the sake of marriage, for the sake of the children. All too often this is at the expense of the health and welfare of the family members, most notably the wives and children, who most often suffer the violence.

As unpleasant as it may be, religious leaders need to recognize what a Cleveland family violence services worker once sadly acknowledged: "Families are the most violent institutions in our society. People are more likely to be victims of violence in their families than on the street—even in the worst part of the city." Pastors need to include this reality in their thinking and planning when they promote the sanctity of marriage. They must recognize that a truly sanctified marriage is one without violence, one in which members do not fear for their welfare or their lives.

The Cycle of Violence

Religious advisers need to accept the fact that when violence occurs in a family it is not an occasional, sporadic event. Research indicates that, if violence has happened once, it is almost certain to happen again. It is usually part of an insidious cycle—the "cycle of violence." This cycle applies most specifically to spouse abuse, but it also has implications for other forms of family violence. Each episode includes three phases: a tension-building phase, an acute battering phase, and a honeymoon phase (Walker 1979:55–70).

The tension-building phase is, just as its name indicates, the period in the family's life when stress is high and tension is increasing. There may be minor incidents of violence, but the family members "walk on eggs" to avoid an explosion. Eventually (this period can last several weeks or even months), the efforts to placate the abuser fail or the potential victims find the tension too great to continue and they will deliberately perform an act to precipitate the violence. "Even the violence is better than the tension." Whatever the immediate cause, the abuser will explode.

When the abuser explodes the acute battering phase begins. During this stage the abuser will totally lose control. This phase involves extreme forms of physical and sexual violence and may last for a few hours or even a few days. At this time the victims may flee or call the police, but most often they will be so terrorized by their attacker that they will stay and accept the beating.

After this violent phase the relationship moves into the honeymoon phase. The violence stops and the abuser—usually the husband—is contrite and sorrowful. He is loving, kind, and apologetic and promises never to be violent again. If the victim— usually the wife—has fled, the abuser will search for her, send her gifts, plead for her to return, and enlist the aid of family and friends to convince her to return and give him another chance. Usually this honeymoon phase is such a reversal of previous behavior and such a uniquely pleasant experience for someone who may have grown up in an abusive home that she decides to try again. The relationship is reestablished. Unfortunately, this merely marks the beginning of a new cycle. Tension again starts to develop, and minor incidents of abuse begin to occur.

Weeks, even months, may pass before the next acute episode of violence, but the reality is that, unless there is outside professional intervention, the violence will indeed recur. Once it has entered a relationship, violence becomes institutionalized within that relationship. Although its frequency can vary greatly, its occurrence is predictable. In some families, it is love and violence (not love and marriage) that "go together like a horse and carriage."

When confronted with families locked in the cycle of violence, religious advisers need to reassess the form of their commitment to the sanctity of marriage. Advisers need to focus on marriage as an institution for the mutual welfare, personal development, and spiritual growth of all the members. They must admit that abusive families are insidious institutions that destroy their members—the abuser as well as the abused—physically, emotionally, and spiritually. Pastors and rabbis must also admit that such marriages cannot be saved merely through more prayer, greater patience, and further sacrifices by the victims, but only by dramatic changes on the part of the abuser.

Accepting such premises means that religious advisers need to reassess their interpretation and application of some critical scriptural passages: those dealing with the place and responsibilities of children in the family, forms of discipline, the role of women in marriage, and the factors involved in the indissolubility of marriage.

Spare the Rod and Spoil the Child

Although the oft-quoted maxim "Spare the rod and spoil the child" is not directly scriptural, there is plenty of biblical basis for such a statement. The book of Proverbs and its Deuterocanonical counterpart, Ecclesiasticus, are great sources of pithy sayings to guide one's daily life, one's family life, and especially the relationship of parents to their children. The advice given seems to favor a strict orientation and to approve of physical discipline. Jesus Ben Sirach, the author of Ecclesiasticus, admonishes his parental readers, "Do you have children? Discipline them, and make them obedient from their youth" (7:23). He also encourages them to be steadfast in their efforts to keep their children in line: "Do not be ashamed . . . of much discipline of children" (42:1, 5).

The scriptural assumption seems to be that children are naturally troublesome and unruly and that they are best brought into line by the rod. "Folly is bound up in the heart of a child, but the rod of discipline drives it far from him" (Prov. 22:15). "The rod and reproof give wisdom, but a child left to himself brings shame to his mother" (Prov. 29:15). Some authors have suggested that the rod referred to is the shepherd's rod and staff, which in Psalm 23 is a source of comfort (Bingham 1986:59). However, the references to this "rod of discipline" seem to be quite frequent and often harsh: "Do not withhold discipline from a child; if you beat him with a rod, he will not die. If you beat him with the rod you will save his life from Sheol" (Prov. 23:13–14). Although the intentions may be good, the use of this rod as described does not sound particularly comforting. The authors of Proverbs and Ecclesiasticus are clear that the purpose of the beatings are for love: "He who spares the rod hates his son, but he who loves him is diligent to discipline him" (Prov. 13:24). "He who loves his son will whip him often" (Ecclus. 30:1). The beatings are nonetheless painful and, unless administered judiciously and with great care, can inflict the physical and psychological harm described in chapters 2 and 3.

The biblical assumption that children are naturally trouble-some has had a long-standing effect on child-rearing practices. Philip Greven in his study of seventeenth- and eighteenth-century parents discovered many of the same principles and documented incredibly harsh and abusive disciplinary tactics which were proudly reported by evangelical pastors. Some of the child-rearing principles that prevailed in that time included this observation by John Robinson: " 'Surely there is in all children, though not alike, a stubbornness, and stoutness of mind arising from natural pride, which must, in the first place, be broken and beaten down; that so the foundation of their education being laid in humility and tractableness, other virtues may, in the time be built thereon.' " To succeed in this, " 'Children's wills and wilful-ness [must] be restrained and repressed' " (Greven 1977:37). As John Wesley put it, " 'Break their wills that you may save their souls' " (Greven 1977:35). This will-breaking, Greven reports, was often accomplished by severe beatings or by long periods of deprivation of food or physical contact. Cotton Mather, on the other hand, "knew that the most effective method for ensuring the compliance of children with the wills of their parents was not beatings but guilt and shame" (Greven 1977:52).

Despite the fact that modern psychology has given us insights into the process of child development that challenge the rationale for such disciplinary practices, many of them are continued today with the same justification. Despite the fact that we have learned that violent discipline only controls unacceptable behavior for as long the threat of violence is present, corporal punishment is still a widely accepted child-rearing practice among all socioeconomic groups in our society. All too often children are told that the beating being administered is "for their own good," that it is being given "so they will learn," or that it is a sign of how much their parents "love" them. No matter how convinced the parents may be of validity of their methods, no matter how well justified the actions may seem to be by scripture, the pain is no less intense and the physical and psychological damage no less enduring.

It is one thing to say that physical discipline should be administered with love and concern for the welfare of the child. It is another to be the recipient of violent beatings administered by Christian parents who justify their actions by the scriptural passages we have just discussed. These admonitions are perceived as justifying the rights of parents to use physical force and reinforcing the obligation of children to honor and respect their parents no matter what treatment they receive from them.

Such an interpretation of the scriptures, and it is one that has not been seriously challenged by most religious leaders, makes it difficult for abused children to look to their church or synagogue for relief from abusive parents. Their awareness of these scriptural maxims, the sermons they may have heard extolling parenthood and admonishing "honor," and their parents' invocations of the proverbs make it difficult for them to acknowledge and discuss the negative and even hostile feelings they may have about their parents.

What is one supposed to do about feelings of anger and resentment when religious authorities say that such feelings, especially toward one's parents, are wrong and sinful? Who does a child go to for help when a pastor or rabbi appears to justify and even praise the very treatment from which the child is seeking relief? How does one discuss one's hostility toward father or mother in a setting that has always extolled parenthood and never acknowledged, at least in sermons, the possibility of abusive parents? What incentive does a boy have to discuss his resentment toward his mother with someone who has only spoken about the rights of parents and the need for children to be controlled, disciplined, and kept in line? What is a young woman seeking assistance from her pastor supposed to do when she is told she is a rebellious teenager who needs more discipline and that she should be more obedient to her parents, who only have her best interests at heart?

In many cases such young people find it necessary for their physical, mental, and even spiritual survival to reject the religious institution which has admonished them to do things, to have feelings, and to express sentiments that a rational response to their experience tells them are contrary to what they should do. They feel they must escape from such a system. They feel that since they cannot live up to 10 percent of the basic rules of the religious institution—the 10 percent that seems to hold special significance—they ought to get out.

What are pastors and rabbis to do in such circumstances? How does one relate to persons who have rejected their religious organization for such reasons? The Judeo-Christian tradition carries a lot of troublesome baggage in the form of apparently insensitive scriptures, a history of rigid application of those scriptures, and a history of institutional unresponsiveness to family violence and the negative experiences of many abused persons.

There are many ways to communicate one's pastoral openness to persons who are suffering or have suffered from family violence. Several of them will be discussed in later chapters. We will look now at one specific way to approach the problem: by achieving a broader understanding of the scriptural understanding of the parental role and parental discipline.

Honor Thy Father and Mother

Probably the most familiar of the Ten Commandments is that which orders children to honor their fathers and mothers. It is the one commandment that most people can quote without hesitation. It is also the only one of the Ten Commandments to which a promise is attached. "Honor your father and your mother, that your days may be long in the land which the LORD your God gives you" (Ex. 20:12).

Both societal awareness and scriptural expression give special emphasis to this commandment. This emphasis is based on the assumption that every child has a unique relationship to his or her parents. This is commonly conceived as a natural obligation, an obligation rooted in the fact of birth. As the author Jesus Ben Sirach put it, "With all your heart honor your father, and do not forget the birth pangs of your mother. Remember that through your parents you were born; and what can you give back to them that equals their gift to you?" (Ecclus. 7:27–28). The realization that one's physical existence stems from one's parents and that the early maintenance of that life depends on nurture and care by parents gives natural weight to the religious admonition to honor one's father and mother. Any thought or action that fails to respect the source of one's life and recognize one's total dependence on one's parents appears to exhibit particularly invidious ingratitude. It seems to go against everything that is good, true, and natural.

The Bible is quick to support that view. The Covenant Codes of the book of Exodus state it clearly: "Whoever strikes his father or his mother shall be put to death" (21:15). Two verses later, the message gets even stronger: "Whoever curses his father or his mother shall be put to death" (21:17). The latter statement is reiterated in Leviticus 20:9. God seems to mean business.

This commandment is frequently reinforced by civil and religious social structures. Many institutions of society are designed to strengthen family life, and in the process they exalt the role of parents. One of the more difficult philosophical issues confronted by those who would prevent child abuse is that of the presumed independence and sanctity of the family. One of the more serious debates revolves around the inherent rights of parents over their children, the right of and the need for parents to discipline their children. When child protection workers intervene in a family, they are frequently accused of interfering with the parents' "God-given rights" to raise and discipline their children as they see fit. Much of the basis for these "rights" is found in Proverbs and Ecclesiasticus.

All the pithy sayings attributed to Solomon and Sirach, no matter how harsh many seem to be, must be understood within the context of the purpose of the Wisdom literature. The Wisdom of the Lord which the books attempt to communicate to foolish humans is based on "the fear of the Lord" which is "glory and pride, and happiness and a crown of joyfulness. . . . [It] will gladden the heart, giving happiness and joy and long life" (Ecclus. 1:11–12). These books of wisdom have been written "that men may know wisdom and instruction, understand words of insight, receive instruction in wise dealing, righteousness, justice, and equity" (Prov. 1:2–3). Abuse and violence are hardly the ways of "wise dealing, righteousness, justice, and equity." The physical harm and psychological devastation associated with violent discipline cannot be reconciled with such purposes.

Parents do need to instruct their children and share with them the insights they will need in later life, but such a process should not produce anguish, anger, and fear. Rather, it should produce "a fair garland for your head, and pendants for your neck" (Prov. 1:9). The various tidbits of child-rearing advice contained in the rest of the books should be understood in this context. To take specific verses out of that loving framework is to distort the intent of the sages who were attempting to provide practical applications for the loving wisdom of God in daily life.

However, to be honest we must recognize that many religiously motivated people have taken the proverbial sayings out of context and used them to justify abusive and domineering behavior. The authors of the Wisdom literature may not have adequately recognized the creative ability of humans to twist otherwise sound advice to justify personal preferences and propensities. They may not have provided adequate controls and correctives for the tendencies of humans—even parents—to use their positions of authority in harmful ways. We are reminded that even absolute parental power can corrupt absolutely.

One of the important messages promulgated by Jesus during his ministry was that all power was to be used in service to others and that the use of any power was to be guided by gentleness, caring, and concern. The apostle Paul recognized that Jesus had offered a new model for relationships between superiors and subordinates. Although unequal relationships do exist and may even serve useful purposes for the good ordering of society, such distinctions between individuals is not a justification for distancing or disdain between people or for the oppression of one person or group by another.

"Every one should remain in the state in which he was called" (1 Cor. 7:20). For Paul that admonition was true even if one was a slave, for that condition was not the determining factor in one's relationship to God or even in one's relationship to one's master. One's social condition could remain the same because what was important was that the nature of the relationship had been changed. The slave should love and serve the master just as the master should love and serve the slave. As oppressive and restrictive as this may seem to us today, Paul believed that what was important was not the social relationship but the way the relationship was lived out in practice (cf. Eph. 6:5–9).

However, if this new kind of relationship, this association dependent not on social standing but on mutual love and concern, was going to work, new guidelines were needed; a new sense of mutuality was necessary. Paul recognized that correctives were required in the standard ways that relationships were then exercised. He recognized that there were excesses and harmful aspects to the way superiors relate to their subordinates, even the way parents relate to their children.

Paul did not deny that children need to obey their parents. "Children, obey your parents in everything, for this pleases the Lord" (Col. 3:20). But he was quick to point out that mutuality is required in this relationship. "Fathers, do not provoke your children, lest they become discouraged" (Col. 3:21). He recognized that it was possible for parents to be excessive in their attempts to discipline their children. They must "bring them up in the discipline and instruction of the Lord," or, as the Jerusalem Bible translates that passage, "correct and guide them as the Lord does" (Eph. 6:4). This is, of course, the same Lord who gave himself unto death for those he loved. Paul is offering a new model for parent-child relationships, a model of gentle, caring love, not abusive, threatening "love." Such a model does not allow for ridicule and denigration, much less beatings and abuse.

It might be well to point out here that we humans have had trouble living up to Paul's ideal for social relationships. We have learned that we could not leave a slave "in the state in which he was called." If slaves and masters were going to have the kind of relationship Paul recommended, their social inequality had to be changed. We humans could not properly manage our power over others.

Unfortunately, we are also learning that in many families the power of parents needs to be controlled externally. It is not safe to leave children "in the state in which [they have been] called."

Such reflections may challenge many long-held beliefs about the integrity of the family, the autonomy of parental power, and the appropriateness of physical discipline within the family. Pastors may need to examine such beliefs and the feelings attendant upon them. This may be a difficult and time-consuming process but it is an important one. If pastors are going to relate to the survivors in their congregations, they must engage in this process. They must seriously examine their assumptions and convictions. Once a pastor has clarified his or her feelings and beliefs about the proper basis for a parent-child relationship, it is time to explore alternatives. He or she can begin to share insights with the congregation, to proclaim the transformed and transforming nature of loving and caring relationships between even subordinates and superiors, to include admonitions regarding parental excesses in Mother's and Father's Day sermons, to make it clear that he or she recognizes the possibility of abuse problems within the congregation.

Such sharing will open the door for discussion and sharing of experiences. It will allow children as well as grown-up abused children to entertain the possibility that their lack of honor and respect for their parents will be understood within the same religious community that admonishes them to "honor your father and your mother."

Wives, Be Subject

Battered women are another group within the web of family violence who have significant problems with some teachings within the Judeo-Christian tradition. The common interpretation and application of both the Hebrew and Christian scriptures affirms the superiority of husbands over their wives. One of the common scriptural words for marriage *(baal)* focuses on the

notion of ownership and lordship. The book of Genesis wastes
little time telling women that your husband "shall rule over
you" (3:16). A favorite Christian passage is Paul's admonition,
"Wives, be subject to your husbands" (Eph. 5:22). Such passages are frequently invoked to justify the rights of husbands to
dominate and control their wives—sometimes even by violent
means.

These passages, combined with those that affirm the sanctity
and indissolubility of marriage—"What therefore God has
joined together, let no man put asunder" (Matt. 19:6)—lay a
heavy burden of guilt on any woman who feels the need to break
out of a violent family setting. She is violating two tenets of her
religion. She is stepping out of her proper role with her husband
and she is breaking up her marriage.

Let us first consider the role of a woman in her family. This
issue is not merely a problem of outdated theology that has long
ago been abandoned or of theology that has been relegated to
extremely conservative, fundamentalist groups. The theology we
are about to discuss is alive and well in mainline Christianity.

A friend who works at a battered women's shelter recently
shared with me a "holy card" that a woman at the shelter had
received from her pastor when she went to him for help. The
card was beautifully printed and laminated. It contained "A
Wife's Daily Prayer" on one side and "Ten Rules for a Happy and
Successful Wife" on the other. The prayer petitioned God for
cheerfulness, unselfishness, patience, and several other laudatory
virtues. The rules were:

1. Avoid arguments. Your husband has his share from other
sources.
2. Don't nag.
3. Don't drink or eat to excess.
4. If you offend your husband, always ask forgiveness before
you retire.
5. Compliment your husband liberally. It makes him a better
husband.
6. Budget wisely together. Live within your income.
7. Be sociable and go out with your husband.
8. Dress neatly and attractively for your husband and keep
your home clean and cheerful.
9. Keep your household troubles to yourself.
10. Pray together and stay together.

The virtues are worthy enough—few of us are opposed to
cheerfulness. Even some of the rules are not half bad. The
problem is that the admonitions are directed only toward the

wife and not to the husband and wife together. The tone of these rules and the way they are directed only at the wife exhibit a patriarchal theology that ought to offend both men and women. As one male, I object particularly to the implications about the delicate male ego contained in the rule to compliment your husband liberally. These rules assume a subservient role for the wife and lack any sensitivity to the mutuality and complementarity that ought to be the basis of a healthy relationship.

What is atrocious about this card is that it was given to a woman who was being battered by her husband. In effect she was being told, Go back to your husband, be cheerful in the face of his beatings, and patiently suffer his abuse. This simple act by a pastor proclaims loudly and clearly an antiwoman theology that condones violence in the family. It is little wonder that many shelter workers accuse Judeo-Christian teachings of contributing to family violence.

When one examines the scriptures, one cannot (and need not) deny that a passage in Genesis says husbands shall rule their wives. However, that line needs to be understood in context; the statement is part of the curse laid upon Adam and Eve for their failure to live up to the requirements of the creation covenant. The statement is not made as part of a blessed promise but as a condemnation brought about by sin. The control of man over woman is the result of a distortion of relationships, not the ideal to be sought in relationships between men and women. Such role relationship is not a blessing for either party.

To understand the ideal to strive for, one need only consider the broader context of the creation story. The two Genesis accounts make it abundantly clear that both man and woman are special creations—"in the image of God he created him; male and female he created them" (Gen. 1:27)—and that they both share much in common, "bone of my bones and flesh of my flesh" (Gen. 2:23). When such unique creatures are bound intimately together, neither is intended to be subordinate to the other and neither ought to be controlled by the other, especially by mutually degrading violence.

Sin may have seriously damaged the ideal relationship that God intended between men and women, but that is not a justification for continuing and furthering the disruption of relationships. The effects of sin are realities in our world, but they do not constitute the ideals by which we ought to guide our lives and form our relationships. The ideal to be affirmed and sought is that of unity and mutuality.

On the other hand, Paul's admonition "Wives, be subject to

your husbands, as to the Lord" (Eph. 5:22) cannot be discounted as part of a curse. He is clearly stating an ideal to be sought. However, what is so often quoted is only part of that ideal. The whole passage speaks about a mutual relationship between husbands and wives, not just a relationship of wives to husbands. The section begins, "Be subject to one another out of reverence for Christ" (Eph. 5:21) and goes on to speak of a mutual relationship between husbands and wives.

It should be noted that the word most commonly translated "subject" would more appropriately be translated "defer" or "accommodate" (Bingham 1986:57). The ideal Paul is trying to communicate is mutual sensitivity and responsiveness, the kind of "more than halfway" willingness to give on the part of both parties that is essential for any successful marriage. Paul goes on to hold up Jesus as the model of giving and service toward which both husbands and wives ought to strive.

Marie Fortune (1983:57) points out that most of Paul's passage on marriage (Eph. 5:21–29) is directed to husbands. "Nine of the verses are directed toward husbands' responsibilities in marriage; only three of the verses refer to wives' responsibilities and one refers to both. Yet contemporary interpretation often focuses only on the wives and often misuses those passages to justify the abuse of wives by their husbands."

It cannot be denied that abuse occurs in many marriages. What cannot be claimed is that Paul in any way condones it. Instead, his recommendation is that "husbands should love their wives as their own bodies. . . . For no man ever hates his own flesh, but nourishes it and cherishes it" (Eph. 5:28–29). In another of his letters Paul indicates that he recognizes the propensity for men of his time to be abusive to their wives. He admonishes, "Husbands, love your wives, and do not be harsh with them" (Col. 3:19).

Paul's ideal of mutual accommodation also extends to the area of sexual relations within marriage. Mutual deference to one another in all matters means that neither member of the marriage relationship has "rights" over the other that are not freely given. Equality and mutuality within marriage mean that all aspects of the relationship, even those related to conjugal relations and sexual access, must be determined by mutual consent. Wives and husbands each have the right to refuse sexual relations. There is a mutual sharing of both rights and duties. As Paul put it, "The husband should give to his wife her conjugal rights, and likewise the wife to her husband. For the wife does not rule over her own body, but the husband does; likewise the husband does not rule over his own body, but the wife does" (1 Cor. 7:3–4).

Thus any rights within marriage are mutual and parallel. They do not exist without the consent of the partner. Persons in a marriage have entered into a unique relationship where all their personal rights are equally shared with and controlled by their marriage partner. They truly are not two but one flesh. The man is admonished to cleave to his wife (Gen. 2:24), not dominate her.

Partners who insist on claiming their personal "rights" without regard for the other's wishes are breaking the unity and mutuality essential to the sacredness of the marriage bond. The bond has been broken because one person has insisted on rights as a separate and distinct person and has ceased to function as part of a larger whole—as a married person.

To summarize, it must be emphasized that the role of a woman in her marriage is not that of an inferior subject who is required to put up with whatever kind of treatment her husband chooses to dish out. She is an equal partner with mutually shared rights as well as responsibilities. She is a "companion" rather than merely a "helper." As Phyllis Trible points out (1978:90), the former concept is a more accurate translation of the Hebrew word *'ēzer* than the more subordinate and inferior concept of helper. As she says, "In the Hebrew scripture, this word *['ēzer]* often describes God as the superior who creates and saves Israel. . . . According to Yahweh God, what the earth creature needs is a companion, one who is neither subordinate nor superior; one who alleviates isolation through identity." If a woman is going to relieve the isolation of her husband, she must be regarded as an equal with important ideas and resources to contribute, not merely as a subservient housewife whose only purpose is to respond to the demands of her husband. She cannot be an equal companion if she is subject to fear and intimidation in her relationship. When the relationship is ruled by threats and violence, the purpose of the relationship has ceased to exist.

Pastors must be careful in their exhortations and admonitions to women about their role in the family. Wives do have an important role and must be accommodating to their husbands. But that accommodation must go both ways. Wives are not to be submissive and subservient, and certainly they must not be the recipients of violence. Nothing in the Judeo-Christian tradition approves of violence directed toward persons, and especially persons committed to the special, loving, and mutual relationship that is marriage.

The Judeo-Christian community has a long way to go to overcome the incomplete and distorted interpretations and applications to which many of the passages of its scriptures have been subjected. Pastors must be clear in their teachings about these passages. Unfortunately, many women feel bound to violent relationships because of the understanding of these passages that they have gained from sermons and admonitions in the past—as well as pastoral exhortations and "holy cards" in the present. In their attempts to live up to what they perceive as the requirements of their faith, they live in constant fear for their lives and well-being. Fear and dread do not constitute the proper role for women in marriage.

The Sanctity of Marriage

But what about the indissolubility of marriage? Does the permanent character of marriage perhaps require that persons, whether male or female, put up with certain fearful and even painful experiences?

Churches and synagogues have long held enviable reputations for maintaining the sanctity of marriage and the family. They have often been the almost solitary bastions of defense for the values of loyalty and commitment within the family. They have upheld marriage as a sacred and permanent covenant.

The roots of such a role and responsibility are found in the creation story. Adam and Eve are formed from a common flesh and are urged to cleave to one another and become one flesh (Gen. 2:23–24). Together they share the beauties of the garden, and together they suffer the results of their common failure.

The Mosaic Covenant that brought the Israelites together as the people of God also affirmed the importance of the family as the basic unit of the new nation. Many of the regulations promulgated to preserve the new community focused on the family (see especially Lev. 20:9–21). Many of the decisions made regarding the distribution of the wealth found in the new land flowing with milk and honey were made according to family grouping. In fact, much of the book of Joshua details this distribution "according to their families."

Since the family is both the basic social unit of any community and the principal source of nurture and support for members of the community, especially its children, it is critical that the family be permanent and stable. The relationship upon which the family is based should not easily be "put asunder." It is understandable that the prophet Malachi would proclaim, "For I hate divorce, says the Lord the God of Israel" (Mal. 2:16). It would make sense for Paul to say, "To the married I give charge, not I but the Lord, that the wife should not separate from her husband . . . and that the husband should not divorce his wife" (1 Cor. 7:10–11), and, "A wife is bound to her husband as long as he lives" (1 Cor. 7:39). Such admonitions make good sense for society and provide sound spiritual direction as well.

When we consider the important role that the family has in the formation of children and in establishing the spiritual climate of a society, we can appreciate the importance of the Rabbinic concept of *Sh'lom Bayit,* peace in the household. Domestic tranquillity is a goal to be sought in every family to foster the proper nurturing of its members.

The important role of the family is not to be denied or in any way minimized. However, the fact of family violence, and particularly spouse abuse, requires that we look closely at what we consider the essence of a family and what truly constitutes a marriage.

A key characteristic of marriage in the Judeo-Christian tradition is faithfulness. The prophet Malachi does not merely proclaim God's displeasure with divorce. The Lord also says, "So take heed to yourselves and do not be faithless" (Mal. 2:16). Jesus' admonition about divorce is made in the context of his concern for the misuse of divorce proceedings for reasons other than unfaithfulness. Paul's advice to married couples is intended to encourage those experiencing difficulties to seek every possible source of reconciliation.

None of these scriptural admonitions insist that marriages be maintained in the face of threats to life and limb for one of the members. Most interpreters of the Judeo-Christian tradition have allowed that special circumstances, most notably the unfaithfulness that has destroyed the basis of a relationship, provide grounds for ending a marriage. The most common "unfaithfulness" thought to justify divorce is adultery. However, we must ask whether family violence is not also a form of unfaithfulness. Does not the abuse that threatens a spouse's life or health constitute a violation of the marriage covenant? It certainly goes a long way toward destroying the trust upon which the relationship ought to be based. As Marie Fortune has put it (1987:34), "If you can't trust your husband not to hit you, what can you trust?"

The reality is that spouse abuse is probably more destructive to the relationship between marriage partners than adultery. It is certainly more devastating to the children whom the family is supposed to be nurturing and protecting. Children are more apt to be aware of violence between their parents than of sexual infidelity. They also are more threatened by the violence because of fear that the next blows may be directed at them—and often they are.

The unity of marriage is an ideal to be sought. No one should "put asunder" the relationship between persons committed to one another in marriage. However, that admonition should be addressed not merely to the battered wife who seeks shelter and counsel about her options; it should be addressed primarily to her abusive husband, who has already sundered the relationship by his violence.

The same principle applies to the ideal of *Sh'lom Bayit.* To accuse a battered wife of destroying domestic tranquillity when she speaks up about the violence she is experiencing is comparable to accusing Jews who complained about the death camps in Nazi Germany of being unpatriotic. The peace in the household has already been destroyed weeks, months, and often years before, when the cycle of violence began. The battered woman seeking help is trying to reestablish truth and integrity in her life. She is attempting to put peace back into her life and the lives of her children. As Rabbi Julie Spitzer puts it (1985:51), *"Sh'lom Bayit* must be held up as an ideal—not as a trap, but as a release. Keeping peace in the home is not a reason to stay in an abusive situation. It is a reason to leave one." Once the cycle of violence has been broken (usually by outside counseling intervention), then the process of rebuilding domestic tranquillity can begin.

As pastors we must recognize that spousal violence undermines the sanctity of marriage and the stability that marriage is supposed to bring to society. If we truly want to foster the religious community's reputation of promoting the sanctity of marriage, we must recognize the reality of violence in marriages and confront the sources of that violence. Only when violence has been eradicated from marriage relationships in our society can we say they have been made sacred.

6

Judge Not: The Pitfalls
of a Moral Response

Pastoral training provides a strong set of moral values and a clear definition of right and wrong. Pastors develop expectations about how they and others are to live. They form strong opinions about what constitutes moral behavior. In particular, they develop a commitment to honesty and truth, to loyalty and family life. They learn to believe in the importance of gentleness and harmony and to advocate the role of forgiveness in maintaining personal relationships. Their training also teaches pastors that part of their job is to impart these moral beliefs to others, to share this value system and to guide others in the ways of goodness and truth.

However, this training may not serve quite so well when a pastor is dealing with persons who have experienced or are experiencing a violent family situation. In fact, this training may be counterproductive, no matter how correct the moral beliefs may be. To focus too early in a relationship with survivors on moral expectations may result in a negative impact on their personal and spiritual growth.

As theoretically appropriate as it may be to expect moral behavior from people, adults abused as children have often grown up with a very different set of expectations and in an environment that required them to protect themselves by methods not necessarily to be considered moral. As important as virtues are, their formation presupposes reciprocity and occurs best in a supportive environment. Persons in violent families never experience such reinforcement. They do not experience loving parents or supportive families. Their experience does not encourage honesty or reward loyalty. For survivors such virtues are not the norm for their lives. In order to survive, they learned actions that are contrary to basic moral principles. They learned a different set of commandments from those promulgated by Judeo-Christian teachings. They may have had to lie and manipulate in order to get care or avoid abuse. Their parents were not persons who merited honor and respect.

To expect forgiveness to be their initial response to abusive parents is to deny the reality of what was done to them. They need to deal with that reality in order to heal the scars which mar their lives. To berate them for their behavior may well convince them that they are not able to live up to the moral expectations or religious beliefs of any church or synagogue. They will become convinced that they do not belong in the company of such respectable and virtuous people. Once again, they will be convinced that they are worthless and evil.

When dealing with behaviors that are traditionally considered unacceptable, pastors must remember that survivors have different experiences about what is plausible, effective, and realistic for their lives. As a result of these experiences, they have developed ways to manage their lives and have formed habits that are deeply ingrained. They consider these ways of operating normal and necessary for their survival. To challenge these modes of operation without fully understanding and appreciating their origin is perceived as criticizing behaviors they consider necessary for their well-being. It denies the validity of their experience. It constitutes a negative judgment on the way they have learned to survive.

This is one context in which Jesus' admonition, "Judge not," is especially important, because such judgments simply reinforce the negative responses survivors received in the past. They constitute another set of statements telling survivors how evil and worthless they are. Such judgments are even more damaging because they negate what the survivors have learned are proper and effective ways to live. It tells them that how they learned to survive is wrong without providing an effective alternative.

In order to help survivors develop the moral responses that our training has taught us to consider good and appropriate, we must initially respect their need to perform as they do. We must recognize the virtue involved in their actions, the value gained from their successful survival in a violent setting. Once we have acknowledged and appreciated this value, then and only then can we begin helping them develop more appropriate and morally acceptable ways to accomplish the same desired ends. Survivors can be taught that the ways they perform are not necessary, or at least not necessary outside their abusive homes. They can learn to obtain what they need and want without resorting to deceit; they can forgive their parents without denying the awful reality of the abuse committed and the psychological and physical damage inflicted.

This response to survivors is consistent with Christian beliefs regarding redemption. A true call for conversion recognizes the unique conditions of the person needing to change. The Christian tradition teaches that God became man in Jesus Christ, and because of that fact God fully understands the unique conditions and limitations of human beings. Thus Jesus' call to conversion is compelling and incontrovertible. It is issued by a human being who understands and appreciates the problems and struggles required when humans try to change their lives.

The religious and moral expectations that commonly cause problems for survivors are twofold. They deal with lying and anger. Religious teachings about these topics often make it difficult for survivors to ask for help. Because the teachings run contrary to their personal experience, they feel they are operating outside the pale of religion's moral expectations. How can we help survivors of family violence determine true morality from distortions and, where appropriate, how can we help them change their responses to ones that are morally acceptable? How can we change the commandments promulgated by their abuse and help them learn a new set?

Lying in Order to Survive

A culture of deception surrounds family violence in our society: Deception and deceit are taught in the family when abusive parents tell their children not to talk about what is happening. Deceit becomes the basis for survival when children are told that, if they say anything, they or other members of their family will be punished. Deception becomes a way of life when an abusive husband tells his wife not to report him "if you know what's good for you," when children hear their mother tell friends there is nothing wrong and that her bruises are the result of an accident. Such children learn early that lying is a way of life.

The range of deception widens when violence is condemned in society but people look the other way and ignore abuse when they see it happening around them. They prefer not to get involved. The deception becomes ingrained when accusations about abuse are rejected without proper investigation and when victims pay higher personal prices than the perpetrators themselves—for example, when children are removed from their homes "for their own good" while the abusive parent remains.

Children learn a distorted sense of truth when their father tells them nothing is wrong even though Mother drinks a lot, burns food, and falls down. Confusion abounds when an uncle who does things that are "not nice" is greeted as a favorite relative. The distortion becomes overwhelming when a mother leaves her daughter alone for long periods of time with a sexually abusive father and then makes snide comments about "Daddy's little girl."

Children learn that lying is a preferred way of life when their parents' demands are so unrealistic and inflexible that the only way they can live up to them is by covering up failures. Children choose to lie when their parents' responses to mistakes are so violent that the only way to avoid beatings is to lie when mistakes are made. Lying is preferred to truth when truth about one's family can result in investigations that may break up the family and put the children in juvenile hall or foster homes.

Children learn to question their perception of reality, their ability to distinguish truth from falsehood, when their experience of violence at home is contrary to the public reputation of the family. They question their own sanity when their attempts to solicit help result in disbelief, accusations of troublemaking, or referral for psychiatric treatment. Under such circumstances, persons in abusive families learn that the deception required to preserve an appearance of family stability and family cohesion is preferred to truth. In such situations children learn to adjust their concept of the family in order to maintain a sense of rationality, of sanity.

Sometimes their perception of family reality becomes so distorted and their experience of family life so far out of sync with the images communicated within society that they are not able to reconcile their images with their experience. These children live in constant confusion about what constitutes truth and reality in their lives.

Even if children are able to understand the truth about the violent realities of their family life, they soon discover that the effort required to express that truth carries a great price. The price of truthfulness turns out to be more than they can bear: personal pain, parental rejection, and family dissolution. As chaotic, disruptive, and distorted as their family may be, it is the only family they have. They do not know what they would do if they lost it.

Such learning of deception easily extends to other areas of their lives and to other relationships. Persons who have learned such distortions in their families have similarly confused perceptions of what is good or bad, true or false, in the broader world. If they cannot figure out what is real in their families, how can they trust their perceptions about other persons, situations, or groups? If deception is a recommended course of action in their families, why should it not be used in other relationships? If certain things are concealed in their family lives, are there not similar things to be concealed in the rest of the world? If some topics are forbidden or unsafe in one circumstance, what makes them okay in another? This thinking is the natural result of the family training grown-up abused children have received, training that has created immense confusion about reality and truth; they have lived with distortion so long they can no longer distinguish truth from falsehood.

When survivors try to tell the truth, they often experience confusion about what really is true. They experience anxiety and even guilt as they fear that they are telling something they are not supposed to, that they are going to get themselves or someone else in trouble. Thus, for them, honesty is not the best policy; it has too many negative ramifications. To expect them to respond positively to a moral exhortation for truthfulness is unrealistic. Any exhortation to honesty must be accompanied by an acknowledgment of the confusion and anxiety that the person may be experiencing as well as help in understanding that the responses they receive from adult authority figures at this time will be different from the responses they got from their parents. Any admonition against lying must be accompanied by the commitment of time and effort necessary to help grown-up abused children sort out truth from falsehood and to convince them that telling the truth is not going to result in tremendous personal cost. They must be convinced that honesty is not going to bring ridicule and beatings and that sharing problems is not going to mean rejection.

All exhortations and admonitions must be accompanied by the acknowledgment that the dishonesty which is being challenged is not perceived as malicious; it is recognized as an act thought to be necessary for survival. Survivors must be convinced that such behavior is no longer necessary, that they are no longer living in dangerous circumstances, and that they are not operating in a volatile environment where a misstatement or an unacceptable response will result in violence. When attempting to convince a survivor that he or she no longer needs to lie for self-protection, you are trying to cast out a prime instrument of self-preservation. You are not asking the survivor to overcome a weakness but to throw out a strong weapon. Such a time-tested tool is not going to be relinquished without a struggle. The abuse survivor must be convinced that it is no longer necessary or that it will not work in normal nonabusive situations.

The world of sports strategy may provide some helpful insights.

A recent column in *Squash News* recommends that when faced with an opponent who has a terrific shot, you have three choices: to avoid, to neutralize, or to attack. You can constantly hit to your opponent's backhand to keep the ball away from a very strong forehand. You can anticipate a strong shot and be prepared to return it, or you can anticipate your opponent's strength and make it an occasion for your own strong return. The last two strategies work well for those who wish to undermine their opponents' confidence in their best shots and force them to rethink their strategy.

Grown-up abused children have learned that lying is one of *their* best shots. Lying is the best way for them to protect themselves and play a winning game of life. Oral chiding alone is not going to convince them to give up such an advantage. They must be convinced that it is not an effective way to win.

Because survivors have learned to lie in a wide range of circumstances, it may be impossible to avoid them all. But if we recognize that they are inclined to lie in many situations, we can anticipate their moves and be prepared to uncover their deception. However, simply uncovering the deception and neutralizing it may not be enough to get them to stop lying. In fact, it may only encourage them to improve their strategy by becoming better liars. We must also be prepared to attack their strength. We must be prepared to uncover their deception in such a way that it not only does not work but works against them and their life goals. They must be helped to understand that lying is no longer effective. If we can destroy their confidence in deception, they can be opened to hearing moral exhortations about the value of honesty. They can develop a new repertoire of shots to play at a new level of human proficiency. They will be able to learn new strategies for dealing with others. Once their confidence in the culture of deception has been broken, they can understand the culture of honesty and respond to moral considerations.

Don't Be Angry

Another issue about which abused children and battered women have moral conflicts with their religious training is anger. Both groups have many reasons to be angry. They have been repeatedly abused and beaten. They have been ridiculed and belittled. Their worth and dignity have been severely maligned. As they work to reassert their value and affirm their life goals, they discover deep reservoirs of anger about the ways they have been treated and the opportunities they have been denied. But, as natural as anger might seem under the circumstances, many believe it is contrary to religious teachings. How often have we been told by religious leaders, "Don't be angry"? We are even told, "Don't feel angry." To do so, we are told, is "wrong," it's "sinful."

It is not hard to find religious admonitions against anger. The Hebrew and Christian scriptures are filled with them.

> A man of quick temper acts foolishly,
> but a man of discretion is patient. . . .
> He who is slow to anger has great understanding,
> but he who has a nasty temper exalts folly. . . .
> He who is slow to anger is better than the mighty,
> and he who rules his spirit than he who takes a city. . . .
> Good sense makes a man slow to anger,
> and it is his glory to overlook an offense.
> Proverbs 14:17, 29; 16:32; 19:11
>
> Be not quick to anger,
> for anger lodges in the bosom of fools.
> Ecclesiastes 7:9

Jesus puts his own special emphasis on the issue of anger when he says, "I say to you that every one who is angry with his brother shall be liable to judgment" (Matt. 5:22).

At face value, those scripture passages seem to confirm that anger is an evil emotion. However, if we read them more closely we recognize that the quotations from Proverbs and Ecclesiastes are not condemning all anger but only hasty anger. They are saying, Be slow to anger. Do not do it without careful consideration and good sense. This is very different from never being or feeling angry at all.

In comparison, Jesus' statement seems considerably more definitive; he seems to be attaching eternal damnation to anger. However, if we look at the Greek text, we discover that Jesus is not condemning all anger. As Andrew Lester points out (1983:45), "The verb *orgizesthai*, translated 'is angry,' is a present participle and refers to continuous action. A more exact translation would be 'everyone who is *continuously* angry' or 'everyone who *keeps on being* angry.'" Jesus is condemning those who *harbor* anger, who allow it to fester in their lives, permeating all of their life and relationships.

Paul in his letter to the Ephesians gives more specific advice concerning anger. When challenging the Ephesian Christians to live up to the fullness of their calling, he says, "Be angry but do not sin; do not let the sun go down on your anger" (4:26). He recognizes the prevalence and even naturalness of anger but says it must not rule one's life.

Of course, that is easy advice to give. When one is sitting quietly at a desk writing, it is easy to say, "Be rational about your anger. Be angry, but not too much. Be angry, but turn the emotion off as soon as the incident is over and be open to reconciliation." We all know that anger is not so easily controlled. Anger by its nature is not purely rational. It is an emotion, and it generates a physiological reaction; adrenaline starts flowing. When we get upset and the adrenaline starts racing through our veins, we do not always feel rational. At the moment of anger we can identify with another of Paul's statements: "I do not understand my own actions. For I do not do what I want, but I do the very thing I hate. . . . I do not do the good I want, but the evil I do not want is what I do" (Rom. 7:15, 19).

If that is the case, wouldn't we all be better off if we simply avoided anger? It can be such a troublesome emotion. It so easily gets out of control. Persons who have lived in abusive families know better than most people exactly how troublesome and destructive anger can be. Many of them have tried to express the anger they felt at their treatment and have suffered further rejection or violence as a result. They have been told they are not supposed to be angry at their parents or their spouse. Their parents or spouse have heaped more abuse on them because they tried to express their feelings about their treatment. As a result they find it easier and safer to follow the standard religious admonition, "Don't be angry!"

As practical as that advice may seem, it usually does not work over the long run. Many of the present problems of survivors stem from repressed anger. It is the source of unexplained tension and anxiety and even some illnesses. Unresolved anger about the past may contribute to drug and alcohol abuse and to irrational and excessive outbursts of anger. This anger is directed at themselves or at persons or situations that do not merit such responses. Misdirected anger can cause serious problems. It can destroy relationships and can even result in lawsuits or criminal prosecution.

Social ethicist Beverly Wildung Harrison expressed this dilemma accurately when she wrote (1985:15):

> We need to recognize that where the evasion of feeling is widespread, anger does not go away or disappear. Rather, in interpersonal life it masks itself as boredom, ennui, low energy, or it expresses itself in passive-aggressive activity or in moralistic self-righteousness and blaming. Anger denied subverts community.

> Anger expressed directly is a mode of taking the other seriously, of caring. The important point is that where feeling is evaded, where anger is hidden or goes unattended, masking itself, there the power of love, the power to act, to deepen relation, atrophies and dies.

Thus trying to deny anger instead of acknowledging it and attempting to deal with the resultant feelings really means that a person remains angry. The anger continues past many sundowns and festers until it breaks forth on a totally inappropriate day and strikes out at someone who does not deserve it. Denial is not, therefore, a "good sense" approach to anger; in fact, it is the way of fools. The way of "great understanding" is to acknowledge anger and to be honest and explicit about it without harming others.

One of the Gospel passages that often makes religious persons uncomfortable—and for which they search for ways to explain away—is the account of Jesus driving the merchants and money-changers from the temple. This story, reported by all four Evangelists (Matt. 21:12–14; Mark 11:15–17; Luke 19:45–48; John 2:14–16), presents a Jesus who is very angry at what he sees being done in the temple. John's Gospel is very careful to make it clear why Jesus got so angry: "Zeal for thy house will consume me" (2:17).

This Gospel story contains a lesson that religious advisers need to remember when dealing with the anger of survivors of abuse. Anger is a necessary and important emotion. It might even be called a virtue, because it is a measure of what a person is zealous about. It would have been a failure on Jesus' part if he had not gotten angry at what he saw happening in the temple. He would have failed to be concerned about the proper use of his "Father's house." His zeal and commitment would have been lacking.

When we are working with persons who are or who have been victims of abuse, we need to be zealous in our anger and in our ability to affirm their anger about their experience. One of the most devastating things about the experience of abuse victims is that they are not allowed to be angry about the way they are being treated. The perpetrators tell them they are not supposed to be angry, and they experience more violence if they do express anger. Soon they feel that anger is not an appropriate response to what is being done to them. Ultimately, they come to believe that they are not worthy of anger, that nothing about them merits such zeal.

If survivors of abuse seek pastoral counseling and again are told not to be angry, they are being told they are not worth caring about. This is not the message we as pastors want to convey. We must accept and even encourage their anger as an appropriate response to the injustice that has been done to them. We must support their feelings and share our own anger about the way they have been mistreated.

Of course, and unfortunately, some survivors of violence are no longer in touch with their anger because they have had to repress it for so many years. They do not know what it feels like to be angry and are even uncomfortable with the thought that they might be angry. They feel anger is wrong.

Such denial of anger may be particularly true for women who have been trained in "mandatory 'niceness'" (Wood 1988:1). They have been so conditioned to be nice girls, to be "sugar and spice and everything nice," that expressing anger has become virtually impossible.

Such an inability to identify and express anger creates a delicate situation for a pastor. He or she must proceed carefully in opening the person to such new emotions. This matter will be discussed at greater length in chapter 9. The important thing to remember at this point is that anger is a legitimate and important virtue. It might be considered a measure of one's spiritual life, a gauge of one's values and commitments. One commitment for all of us ought to be a zeal for an end to family violence in our society.

Even if we accept anger as a virtue (remember, Paul did advise his Ephesian Christians to "be angry"), that does not mean anger should become a way of life. Righteous anger, anger properly directed at an injustice, is an appropriate response to abuse, but it should not become all-consuming. Although anger is a healthy response to victimization and an important part of a survivor's reaffirmation of dignity, it must be managed with great understanding and discretion. (See the discussion of anger in chapter 9.)

That task, the task of managing the conflicts of life and growing in virtue, is a challenge which faces all persons who are serious about their spiritual life. For survivors, spiritual growth presents specific difficulties. The question of how one can be angry and also love one's neighbor, forgive one's enemies, and grow spiritually is only one question among many.

7

Spirituality
for Survivors

The title of a short book by Josef Goldbrunner, *Holiness Is Wholeness,* has provided a guiding principle for my own spiritual life as well as the guidance I have offered others. I have sought for and tried to help others develop a life-style that is personally integral and complete as well as congruous with other persons and creation. I have sought to foster life guided by the "plumb line" of the Lord (Amos 7:7–9) and filled with the abundance promised by God through Jesus Christ.

Persons who live in violent families do not experience life as either whole or abundant. Their lives have been painful, cruel, and unfair. Therefore, many survivors are physically, mentally, emotionally, and spiritually stunted, maimed, and deformed. Rather than being hopeful, courageous, and confident, they are frightened, bitter, and frustrated, depressed, angry, and self-deprecating—hardly the basis for a strong and enriching spiritual life.

This book has focused, thus far, on the struggle by survivors for wholeness. We will now focus on forms of spiritual guidance that can be helpful for survivors and on resources they can draw on for the hope, courage, and confidence necessary for holiness as well as wholeness.

Spirituality for survivors is a topic that needs much work in the future. The traditional content and processes of spiritual direction need to be adapted for survivors of family violence. As pastors, spiritual directors, and survivors themselves read this chapter, I ask them to reflect on their own experiences. Am I accurate? What needs to be discarded? What needs to be revised? Let me hear from you. Maybe this chapter can initiate a dialogue about spiritual direction for survivors that can produce helpful insights beyond this preliminary effort.

The content for this chapter has come from several sources. Members of Grown-Up Abused Children groups have shared the spiritual exercises that have been helpful for them. I have suggested spiritual approaches to persons individually or within groups. My counselees have been honest enough to let me know what works and what does not; I thank them for the insights they have provided. I spoke with former group members whose prayer life is especially strong and helpful to them; I appreciate their time and openness. I have also read and reflected to find appropriate spiritual guidelines for the survivors with whom I have been privileged to work.

Two authors' approaches to spiritual life have been especially helpful, Henri J. M. Nouwen and Matthew Fox. What distinguishes their work is their positive developmental approach, as opposed to a negative focus on overcoming evil and sin. Survivors do not need an emphasis on evil and sin; they have gotten more than enough of that. As victims they were constantly told how wicked and bad they were, and as survivors they are struggling to overcome that image. They also do not need to be told to suppress their pride. Most have so little self-confidence that for them pride is not a deadly sin, it is an impossibility. Their self-esteem is too damaged for them to suffer from arrogance. Survivors do not need lectures on asceticism and mortification. They have been sufficiently humiliated and mortified by members of their families.

Henri J. M. Nouwen has described spiritual life as a movement from loneliness to solitude, hostility to hospitality, and illusion to prayer. Solitude, hospitality, and prayer are not ends in themselves but means to the fullness of life in and with God. The goal is a new life that enables one to love oneself, others, all of creation, and the Creator with joy and fulfillment. Solitude, hospitality, and prayer are steps along the way to new life, to a holiness which is wholeness. I will focus on five areas of special concern for the spiritual growth of survivors. They are the relationship between hope, faith, and trust; forgiveness; the problems with the concept of a "fatherly" God; the meaning of suffering; and the role of prayer.

Hope, Faith, and Trust

Nouwen's first step in spiritual growth is the movement from loneliness to solitude, from being uncomfortable and anxious within oneself to inner peace. For a survivor, a key impediment to progress in spiritual growth is fear. Nouwen says (1975:16) that "the roots of loneliness . . . find their food in the suspicion that there is no one who cares and offers love without conditions, and no place where we can be vulnerable without being used." For survivors of family violence, that suspicion was confirmed in their families from infancy. Fear of those closest to them has instilled loneliness, created isolation, and imposed silence.

Theirs was not a quiet silence which fosters reflection, but one filled with the noise of anxiety, depression, and frightening images. Nouwen says (p. 28) that to turn loneliness into solitude one must love the questions which life has presented and pay attention to the innermost self worthy of love. For survivors, their innermost self has been declared unworthy of love and the questions of life have challenged the very value of their existence.

Nouwen maintains (p. 43) that "the beginning of healing is in the solidarity with the pain" of life. For survivors, this pain is physically real and personal. To confront it means they must confront all the distrust and suspicion, even of themselves, which they have been taught so effectively throughout their lives. Since this distrust is so deeply ingrained, dealing with it is a difficult and frightening task. Therefore, the initial focus of spiritual growth for survivors must be on calling forth their hope, affirming their faith, and reinforcing their trust.

If survivors are to achieve spiritual healing, they must be strengthened to recognize the possibility for new life. They must be convinced that they can be "delivered from the hand of those who enslaved them," can "break the bars of their yoke" and can "dwell securely" in their home (Ezek. 34:25–31). This does not come naturally.

In a special way, survivors are people of hope. The common blessings of life (security, acceptance, and love) are for them "as yet unseen." For them, justice and peace have never reigned, even in the family that ought to have been their source of comfort. They are still seeking a home in which they can live in safety.

Walter Brueggemann points out in his book *Hope Within History* that hope is the virtue primarily of those who do not possess the blessings and power of this world that make one satisfied and complacent. Hope is the virtue of those who see the imperfection of the present, who recognize the fear, insecurities, and inequalities that exist, and who work for a new order of things. This recognition of imperfection and its articulation are critical aspects of hope, because *"hope emerges among those who publicly articulate and process their grief over their suffering"* (Brueggemann 1987:84).

Spiritual directors must help survivors articulate their pain because "the first enemy of hope is *silence, civility, and repression*" (ibid., p. 88). To enable survivors to speak their pain is to enable them to break out of loneliness and believe that the questions and anxieties of life can be resolved. Then they can experience that faith which is "the assurance of things hoped for, the conviction of things not seen" (Heb. 11:1).

Matthew Fox, the leading spokesperson for Creation Centered Spirituality, maintains that faith and trust are closely allied. He says (1983:83), "Trust is not just a psychological issue—it is in fact a faith issue, indeed *the* faith issue." He points out that the scriptural word traditionally translated as "faith," and commonly understood as "intellectual assent," in fact means "trust."

Spiritual directors for survivors of abuse must seek to instill in them a faith and trust in themselves and their potential for growth, a trust in their anger as a measure of injustice, and a trust in their own anguish as a call for new direction in their lives. This trust can enable survivors to celebrate their dignity and self-worth. It can enable survivors to fulfill the prerequisite for Jesus' second great commandment. They will learn to love themselves so they can "love . . . your neighbor as yourself" (Luke 10:27). They will be reconciled to themselves, freed from self-hate, and enabled to feel compassion for themselves. Then they can recognize and trust a caring God. This trust can heal. It can cast out fear.

When trust and self-respect are achieved, survivors can achieve the inner quiet necessary to convert the loneliness and isolation, which dominated their lives as victims, into solitude and inner peace. They can hear the questions of their lives through the din of their anxieties. They can let go of the negative images imposed on them by abusers and acknowledge the pain in their lives, so they can be liberated from it rather than controlled by it. They can be released from fear of their abusers and freed to forgive them.

Forgiveness

Nouwen describes the second movement as "a painful search for a hospitable place where life can be lived without fear and where community can be found" (1975:46). For survivors, this search has gone on for years. It was forced upon them within the confines of their home—the place to which one normally turns for hospitality. Therefore, they carry with them deep hostility—most often directed toward their parents or spouses. To be able to receive others in hospitality, they must learn to forgive their abusers.

Once when I was starting a new Grown-Up Abused Children

group, an incident occurred that illustrates the depth of this problem. As the members settled in their places, one woman, whom I'll call Linda, broke in before I could bring the group to order. "I have a question before we start," she said. "Are you going to tell me I have to forgive my mother for what she did? If you're going to tell me to forgive and forget, I'm not staying."

The theological and spiritual issue of forgiveness had never been put to me quite so bluntly. "No," I replied, after some quick reflection, "I'm not going to tell you to forgive your mother. My first concern is that you get in touch with what happened to you as a child and how you feel about it. I'm certain one of your major feelings will be anger, which is very appropriate. As you determine what you want to do about that anger, you may want to confront your mother. She may apologize and ask for forgiveness. Then you will have to decide whether you want to forgive her. I'm certainly not going to encourage you to forgive and forget. I want you to remember what happened to you. Then, and only then, can you decide about forgiveness."

"I can accept that," Linda said, settling back in her chair. "I'll stay."

Linda participated in the group for several months. During those months she discussed her feelings toward her mother at great length. She had some angry simulated conversations, but she never had the opportunity to confront her mother in person about the abuse. However, as Linda dealt with her feelings about her past, she became more gentle in her attitudes. We never discussed the issue in theological terms again, but Linda did develop an attitude of forgiveness toward her mother and experienced greater peace concerning their relationship.

This story exemplifies the spiritual problem that those who have been abused confront when seeking pastoral guidance. All too often, the first thing they are told is to forgive and forget. They are reminded that God forgives us for our many offenses, that Jesus said we should forgive our brother "seventy times seven" (Matt. 18:21–22), and that on the cross Jesus forgave his executioners "for they know not what they do" (Luke 23:34).

Such admonitions seem hollow and insensitive to women who have forgiven their assaultive husbands the allotted four hundred ninety times, only to be beaten again. They seem totally out of touch with reality for young people who want desperately to forgive their parents and establish a safe, caring relationship but are constantly rebuffed. Grown-up abused children dream of living in a loving family where the pains of the past can be forgiven, but when the problems of the past are discussed, their parents deny them, say the problems are exaggerated, or declare that the children "only got what they deserved."

For survivors, forgiveness can be an empty and even a dangerous virtue. Forgiveness that forgets puts a battered wife or child back into the very environment that caused them harm. It re-creates the circumstances that allowed the offender to abuse them. To recommend such forgiveness is dangerous.

Even if abused children have moved away from their parents and battered wives have separated from their husbands and are no longer in danger of further abuse, to ask them to forgive is to deny the reality of the violence and injustice done to them; to advise forgetfulness is to fail to be zealous about the dignity of the person who has been abused.

Such an approach also denies the complex and dialogic nature of forgiveness. It forgets what Alan Richardson (1950:86) tells us about the scriptural notion of forgiveness: "Forgiveness is throughout conditional upon repentance, a word which quite clearly in its OT and NT equivalents involves a change of mind and intention."

Forgiveness that takes repentance seriously involves dealing with the awful reality of what has been done. Children have been abused. Wives have been battered. Relationships have been shattered. Forgiveness in such circumstances demands that the harsh realities of pain, hurt, and violence—both physical and psychological—be taken seriously. It does not allow denying what happened or turning an offense into a nonoffense. Rather it means saying clearly, "That was wrong. That hurt me. But if you are willing to change, to really do things differently, I will forgive you."

Such an approach is consistent with the biblical notion of repentance, which demands a complete change, a total reorientation in the way one lives. " 'Repent' in its NT usage implies much more than a mere 'change of mind'; it involves a whole reorientation of the personality, a 'conversion' " (Richardson 1950:192). In the case of a violent parent or spouse this means they must admit they have been abusive (something that many never do) and they must get outside help to control their behavior. Outside help is essential, because research indicates it is virtually impossible for abusive parents or spouses to break the cycle of violence without professional intervention (cf. Walker 1979:28–29). Thus the acceptance of such assistance is an essential part of the act of repentance. It is a part of the reorientation of personality necessary for true conversion. Without it, there is no repentance and there can be no forgiveness in the biblical sense of the term.

This does not mean that the survivor is not willing to forgive, nor does it mean that the abused child or battered wife bears a continuous grudge or festering anger toward the abuser. The battered wife can develop an attitude of forgiveness. She may be able to acknowledge the validity of her anger and then let it go so she can move on with her life. She may admit the humanness of her batterer and even recognize the experiences in his life that contributed to his abusive behavior, but, if he is unwilling truly to repent, to accept his responsibility, to change his life, she is not able to complete the dialogue of forgiveness. She certainly should not forget what he has done; that would be extremely dangerous.

A survivor may be more than willing to follow Jesus' admonition, "If your brother sins, rebuke him, and if he repents, forgive him" (Luke 17:3). However, she may also be confronted with the reality which Jesus acknowledged when he said;

> If your brother sins against you, go and tell him his fault, between you and him alone. . . . But if he does not listen, take one or two others along with you, that every word may be confirmed by the evidence of two or three witnesses. If he refuses to listen to them, tell it to the church; and if he refuses to listen even to the church, let him be to you as a Gentile and a tax collector.
>
> Matthew 18:15–17

Survivors confronted with an unrepentant abuser—and, unfortunately, many of them are—are faced with the task of resolving their anger and hurt without the prospect of true forgiveness. They are consigned the task of developing an attitude of forgiveness without the help of the dialogue that can result in reconciliation. They must struggle to determine the appropriateness of their feelings without any admission of guilt on the part of the offender. Such a situation makes the process much more difficult. Survivors must struggle alone to understand experiences that defy comprehension. They must give perspective and order to events that were inherently irrational.

With these pressures working against them, how are survivors to resolve their anger and express forgiveness? How are they to move toward hospitality? If real forgiveness and reconciliation are not possibilities, what are survivors to do? How can they move beyond their frustration, resentment, and pain? How can a pastor help a survivor let go of anger, develop an attitude of forgiveness, and become open to the possibility of reconciliation when the option of fulfillment is not available?

A pastor must allow the survivors to follow their own schedule. As important as letting go of anger and becoming open to forgiveness are for healing and wholeness, they are not the first responses open to a person who has suffered abuse. Such responses cannot be called forth on cue.

Developing an attitude of forgiveness is a process that differs in intensity and duration, depending on each person's personality and the extent of the abuse. It is a complex and highly personal process. It cannot be accomplished according to someone else's timetable. For a pastor to expect a battered wife or abused child to attain a high level of insight and objectivity in a short time is unrealistic at best and insensitive and demeaning at worst.

Developing an attitude of forgiveness is not an act of the will accomplished at a specific moment, but rather a series of steps, a complex procedure that involves several stages. Sidney and Suzanne Simon (1987:4) have identified six stages in what they call "forgiveness work": denial, self-blame, victim, indignation, survivor, and integration. These stages often overlap, are not necessarily consecutive or linear, and can take several years.

The Simons are clear about the importance of anger, "indignation," as part of the healing process of forgiveness. To deny a survivor's right to anger as a part of the healing process is not only to steal the person's dignity but also, as we have seen, to short-circuit the healing process and restrict the possibilities for growth. Anger is a necessary step, enabling the survivor to let go of the abuse experience and attain inner peace. Marie Fortune quotes a survivor who has attained such peace (1983:209): "I will not let it continue to make me feel bad about myself. I will not let it limit my ability to love and trust others in my life. I will not let my memory of the experience continue to victimize and control me." Matthew Fox has said (1983:163), "Forgiveness is another word for letting go. . . . Forgiveness is about letting go of guilt—some imagined, some real—and about letting go of fear."

Forgiveness that lets go does not condone the violence done. It does not even forget it. It simply creates an attitude that allows the victim, now a survivor, to acknowledge anger but move beyond it to a new personal awareness. A battered wife, for example, recognizes the reality of her abusive past but also recognizes that the experience is over. She has grown to know herself as much more than her abusive past. As she moves beyond her anger, she is no longer dominated by her abuser or even by her desire for retaliation. She is open to forgive her batterer, if he ever comes to her in repentance.

That special moment when repentance and forgiveness unite in reconciliation may be a long time coming. It involves a lengthy and complicated process for both parties. However, if pastors are to enable such reconciliation, they must remember that both need to be involved. It is not enough to tell a battered woman or abused child to forgive; the abuser must also be told to repent.

In this process, both persons must be dealt with separately; reconciliation cannot be accomplished through "family counseling." The disparity in power in an abusive family is so profound that it is unrealistic to expect joint counseling to uncover the underlying conflicts within the relationship. The problems involved in working with an abuser are so complicated they should only be addressed by a specially trained counselor.

Pastors who are not so trained should avoid trying to solve the problems of abusers and their victims. Nevertheless, they should support survivors in their search for safety, sanity, and sanctity. They can confront the abusers about their violence and not let them excuse and deny it. As both parties seek expert help, clergy can be a pastoral force in eventually bringing the reformed penitent and the healed survivor together in reconciliation. Reconciliation with one's converted abuser can be the ultimate challenge of hospitality for a survivor.

A Fatherly God?

Noisy loneliness may be turned to peaceful solitude and raging hostility to forgiving hospitality, but significant spiritual challenges still remain for survivors, as they are called to reach out to a God who is identified as a caring Father. This image raises two problems. Since their experience of a father or parent has not been positive, they are not clear to whom they are relating. Furthermore, if God cares for them, why have they suffered so deeply? These are two of the problems survivors must confront before they can move to prayer.

Many survivors find it difficult to get very excited about belief in a God who is addressed as Father. They cannot respond to such a concept because the notion of fatherhood generates feelings of revulsion, not respect; anger, not attraction; and anxiety, rather than enthusiasm. Since the concept of the Fatherhood of God seems integral to the Judeo-Christian tradition, they are confronted with a problem of belief and spirituality.

For many the description of God as Father results in no belief in God at all. If a key element of divinity is loving fatherhood, they lack any experience with which to connect the concept. Since they had no experience of a caring parent or loving father, they cannot conceive of a supreme Caring Parent or Loving Father whom they might honor or turn to in times of need.

This problem is not limited to those who experienced abuse from their fathers. Despite the fact that the Judeo-Christian tradition has been restrictive in its use of masculine images for

God and has ignored the feminine images that put God in the role of a loving mother, merely correcting this distortion will not solve the problem for survivors. For them, the reality was they were not safe in their homes. Whichever parent may have been abusive, the other was not protective and caring either. Their basic experience was fear and danger in that place which ought to have been safe and comforting. Whatever the gender of their abuser, they do not understand the concept of a parental figure who cares for and protects them.

John, a member of a Grown-Up Abused Children group, was adamant about his atheism. He insisted that the concept of God was phony. We assured him that belief in God was not required for participation in the group. During the next several months the topic was never a part of any of our discussions. Nevertheless, during those months John opened himself to the caring of the group members. One day he confided to me that now he at least allowed for the possibility of a God. As several more months passed, John became convinced there was indeed a God—who had become an important part of his life.

This "conversion" was not the result of a rational apologetic but rather of loving, caring relationships. The constant anger and violence in John's family had not produced any experience of love to which he could connect the religious beliefs he heard discussed in church. The fear and distrust of others engendered by his family had deprived him of the possibility of experiencing love anywhere else. It was only after experiencing care from members of the group that John was able to learn the human trust necessary for religious belief and faith. Without such human experience as a basis for religious experience, faith was not accessible to him.

Not all persons who have experienced abuse become confirmed atheists. They may still believe in God, but their concepts may lack much of what most people committed to the Judeo-Christian tradition consider important and meaningful—a loving, personal God. A survivor's concept of God may be that of a stern taskmaster who is demanding and impossible to please. For them God is another force in their lives waiting for them to make a mistake for which they can be punished.

Even if their concept of God is not totally negative and demanding, it often lacks personality and tenderness. Because they lack the experience to which they can connect what for many is a key attribute of God, that of a loving parent, their relationship to God lacks any personal character or tenderness. They are functional atheists because their belief lacks anything personal, sensitive, and enlivening. They have no basis from which to call forth a joyful response to a caring God. They find it difficult to enter into a loving relationship with a loving God.

For these survivors their spirituality, like their lives, lacks the joy, warmth, and tenderness that grow out of trusting, caring relationships. Put another way, because they never experienced trust and caring, their life and its transcendent expression, spirituality, lack the warmth and gentleness which are the basis for true joy.

Proclaiming God as a loving Father or extolling the blessings of a fatherly God will not attract, entice, or convince survivors to explore the riches of a life of faith. They are not able to open their lives easily to the blessings, richness, and fulfillment available through opening themselves to a loving God. They also find it difficult to respond to any call for a relationship of love. Such persons were assured by their parents that they were loved, but they found that this love entailed threats, pain, and abuse. Like John, they must first experience human love, caring, and protection in order to relate to the religious concept of a loving parent. Nouwen himself acknowledges (1975:92) that "we come to the growing awareness that we can love only because we have been loved first." A sensitive religious community is important to the spiritual growth of survivors.

Not all survivors reject God as an alien concept. Some persons turn to God as Father from early childhood as a source of comfort and consolation. They are able to separate the violence of their parents from the notion of a loving God who cares for and sustains them. Some survivors tell of seeking out churches during their childhood as places where they felt safe and where they could speak to someone whom they knew loved them. Such times provided precious moments of security and peace. Their spiritual relationship with God the Father compensated for their lack of a caring family.

Suffering

A problem closely related to survivors' problems with the concept of a fatherly God is the issue of a God who allows suffering. Survivors of family violence have often suffered terribly for many years. Pain and fear have been constants in their lives, even from the innocence of their infancy. The questions, "Why is this happening to me?" "What have I done to deserve this?" "Why does God allow this?" have been a regular part of their struggle. For many, their failure to find satisfactory answers results in a crisis of faith.

The fact of suffering in the world has created crises of faith for believers from time immemorial. Many sensitive and profound examinations of this classic theological problem have been made by better minds than mine. I do not presume to have special answers to this problem. My goal is to articulate some specifics as they relate to the spiritual struggle of survivors and to point out responses that are *not* helpful. I will also suggest pastoral responses that may help survivors resolve their faith conflicts and the anger they may feel toward God.

Christians frequently resolve their conflicts around personal suffering by referring to the example of Jesus' sacrificial death. The example of Jesus, the suffering servant who "learned obedience through what he suffered" (Heb. 5:8) and who "humbled himself and became obedient unto death, even death on a cross" (Phil. 2:8), is often the object of reflection and meditation. His example is a strong image that can give meaning, purpose, and dignity to one's personal suffering. As has been said previously about anger and forgiveness, some religious solutions cannot be imposed upon survivors by persons outside themselves. These conclusions must be reached according to one's own timetable.

All too often, Jesus as the suffering servant is held up as a model for a person suffering family violence. The most famous example of this is John Calvin. His admonition to a battered woman is well known among religious persons working in the domestic violence field. Although Calvin had "special sympathy for women who are evilly and roughly treated by their husbands," he could not find himself "permitted by the Word of God . . . to advise a woman to leave her husband." Instead, he exhorted her to "bear with patience the cross which God has seen fit to place upon her; and meanwhile not to deviate from the duty which she has before God to please her husband, but to be faithful whatever happens" (quoted in Bussert 1986:12).

Such advice is not helpful; it is dangerous. Research on family violence indicates that patient suffering does not lessen the level or frequency of violence. Often the violence merely escalates. What is the value of this continued suffering? Who is being redeemed by it? Whose salvation is being accomplished?

Certainly not the batterer. If he is going to change his behavior, he must be confronted by a demand to stop his violence, not allowed to continue it unchallenged. He must be called to repentance, not confirmed in his violence by silence and acquiescence.

The children in a family where there is spouse abuse are not redeemed by allowing the violence to continue or by keeping the family together "for the sake of the children." Lenore Walker (1979:30) reports that, in families where there is violence between spouses, the children often have emotional and educational problems and frequently are targets of abuse by the violent parent. The Children's Defense Fund reports (1988:7), "It is estimated that about 40 percent of the children of victims of spousal abuse are also abused."

The battered wife or abused child is not being redeemed by being victimized. A person may choose to be in a position that results in suffering for a higher good. But abuse in one's family does not serve any noble purpose. As Marie Fortune states bluntly (1983:197), such abuse "is not chosen and serves no greater good."

Victims of family violence should not be told to simply "bear their crosses." Even Jesus' suffering and death on the cross was not redemptive because it was painful. If Jesus had merely suffered and died, his violent death would have been meaningless. Its redemptive value was made possible through his resurrection. Jesus' resurrection proclaims for Christians of all time that pain and suffering and death need not be controlling factors in our lives but must and can be challenged and overcome. To preach a "theology of the cross" that fails to include the resurrection is to advocate a theology of death without the promise of new life. All too often, abuse victims are admonished to accept a theology of the cross that does not promise them new life, and certainly not abundant life (cf. John 10:10).

Abuse victims do not need to be exhorted to greater patience. Most of them suffered patiently for years before they came forward for assistance. They do not need more suffering to "build their character." Their character has already been deeply scarred by violence. To suggest that the abuse they are experiencing is a punishment for some past sin is, at best, simplistic and fatalistic. Such an explanation reinforces the low self-image common to survivors. It also reaffirms the notion of a harsh and vengeful God, which is already a problem for persons experiencing abuse in their families. Such explanations increase a survivor's sense of abandonment by God. The Judeo-Christian tradition needs to affirm two primary images that can have profound implications for persons who suffer from family violence: the exodus and the resurrection.

Just as the God of Abraham, Isaac, and Jacob saw fit to free the Israelite nation from the suffering and oppression of slavery, that same God proclaims liberation for those bound by the terrors of violence in their families. Those who profess to be followers of that liberating God must announce the possibility of freedom to those in their congregations who are presently enslaved by abuse.

The Christian church also needs to proclaim the power of Jesus' resurrection as a message to guide the lives of persons who have suffered abuse. Such persons need to hear about that power which overcame Jesus' total vulnerability and terrible suffering. They need to learn that they too have the possibility for a new life; that they can move beyond being a victim to the new life of a survivor. Healing and wholeness are possible beyond the abuse they have suffered.

Pastors would do well to remember that the exemplary wife and mother of the Gospels once proclaimed that the mighty should be "put down" and the lowly "exalted" (Luke 1:52). Jesus began his public ministry by announcing "release to the captives and . . . liberty [for] those who are oppressed" (Luke 4:18), and he regularly reminded his followers that those in power should be servants (Luke 22:24–27). The Gospels do not encourage violence and oppression, and they do not exalt suffering as an end in itself. Violence, oppression, and suffering are to be eradicated; they are not virtues to be promoted. The good news of the Gospel for battered women, abused children, and all others who suffer unjustly is that God does not intend suffering and there is hope for liberation from oppression. This must be the message we proclaim to victims and survivors alike—churches and synagogues can aid in freeing these people from family violence and its effects.

The liberating power of the exodus and the resurrection must be proclaimed to survivors. These events in Jewish and Christian history did not erase what had gone before—degrading slavery and violent death. They moved beyond those limiting and devastating experiences to a new land and a new life. The people affected—Moses and the Israelite nation and Jesus and his disciples—were called to community and to courage.

Family violence has a deadening effect not only on those who suffer the violence but also on society as a whole. Unmasking the illusion of familial bliss can be a profound spiritual experience for both religious communities and the survivors in their midst. Naming this senseless reality and rising above it will not lessen the pain of the victims, but it can provide survivors with the strength to forgive and all persons with the opportunity to love. The virtues of love and forgiveness are, as Rabbi Harold Kushner has said (1981:148), "The weapons God has given us to enable us to live fully, bravely, and meaningfully in this less-than-perfect world." This is the principal challenge for all the saints of God.

Prayer

Once survivors have resolved their conflicts with violent and vengeful images of God, are they ready for the abundant life that can be found in prayer? Are they ready to open their minds and hearts to God? Yes and no.

Survivors may be in a better position than most people to develop a strong spiritual life. Henri Nouwen maintains (1975:80) that "it is only in the lasting effort to unmask the illusions of our existence that a real spiritual life is possible. [We] need the willingness and courage to reach out far beyond the limitations of our fragile and finite existence toward our loving God in whom all life is anchored."

Survivors have been freed from the confining images of human immortality and power. Few human illusions have survived their abusive experiences. They know the precariousness of existence, because they have lived in fragile and even life-threatening environments. They learned that life is not fair and that there are no guarantees. They have experienced vulnerability and faced death; they have looked over the edge of nothingness. They are empty and ready for the enlivening power of God. In the words of Matthew Fox (1983:172), they are emptied so they are "vulnerable to beauty and truth, to justice and compassion . . . truly hollow and hallowed channel[s] for divine grace."

Survivors may be empty of human pretensions and their minds may not be cluttered with human aspirations, but they may instead be ridden with guilt and their minds filled with frightening images. Their abusive experiences have removed all semblance of pride, all self-satisfaction, but those same experiences have added layers of fear and instilled images of terror.

In order for their minds to be truly open so that God can be known to them, a special kind of cleansing, a special form of centering, will be necessary. The fears and anxieties generated in their families still intrude on their moments of contemplation, stifle the silence in their hearts, and fill their solitude with distress and despair. They cannot focus on anything but the fear and guilt they feel. The anxiety generated by their past floods the present, and they cannot turn to God in trusting prayer.

One woman said that every time she attempted prayer she felt as if she were being swallowed by a whirlpool. Each time she tried to pray, she had to pass through this fear before she could focus on her meditation. Other survivors describe a sensation of having holes in their bodies, which they believe contain frightening images. Before they can center themselves in prayer, they must confront the images and reestablish their wholeness and value.

Therefore, the first step for spiritual directors of survivors is not to cleanse them from pride and self-satisfaction but to free them from anxiety and despair, to relieve them of their tensions and fears. Spiritual directors must acquaint survivors with the physical mechanics of prayer and meditation. They must teach them techniques of breathing and relaxation. In many cases, they will have to lead them through the steps of relaxation procedures. They must help them learn to focus their attention on a single word or short phrase. They will have to teach visualization techniques by which survivors can confront the fearful images within themselves, release the tension that binds them, and fill the gaps they feel.

Such training demands more than the learning of techniques. Those techniques must be used to accept the darkness and pain of their lives, to embrace the desert of the exodus and the despair of the cross. Survivors must learn that even as they affirm the blessed creation of which they are a part, they must also acknowledge the "groaning in travail" (Rom. 8:22) that is part of that gift. Even as they feel overwhelmed by darkness, they must remember that "darkness is not dark to [God], the night is bright as the day; for darkness is as light with [God]" (Ps. 139:12). Their healing and their spiritual growth come from confronting their anxiety.

Henri Nouwen points out (1975:89) that the Latin word for anxiety is *angustia,* which means narrowness. By overcoming the anxiety (narrowness) imposed upon them, survivors will confront the questions life has presented (an important part of the first movement of the spiritual life), let go of their anger (the forgiveness involved in the second movement), and be freed to receive new life from the God of all life. They will have achieved the holiness that enables them to embrace the whole of life—the abundant life to which they had been called but of which they had been deprived by family violence.

8

Being All Things
to All Survivors

Parishes and synagogues are natural and appropriate places to deal with issues related to family violence. They are frequent gathering places for families. Most are located in residential areas, are organized around family schedules, and focus on the family as their primary unit. Churches and synagogues are so well organized to serve the needs of families that single persons often complain they are being left out or ignored.

The issues raised by family violence and the problems created by abuse are also natural issues for pastoral care because they deal with the critical areas of self-esteem, repentance and reconciliation, and the spiritual growth of persons as they strive to overcome the harshness of their lives. However, many pastors report that they never hear about family violence from the members of their congregation and are never called upon to deal with these issues. Based on this absence of reported problems and requests for help, their sense is that the problem does not exist.

However, statistics would suggest that it is practically impossible for a congregation not to have members who are experiencing or at sometime have experienced one of the forms of family violence. The problem is so prevalent that no component of our society is unaffected. Those pastors who make a concerted effort to be sensitive to the issues of family violence and let their congregations know of their concerns report a tremendous increase in the number of persons seeking their aid. Marie Fortune (1983:17) tells of a pastor who, during the course of participating in a several-weeks workshop on family violence, experienced a tremendous increase in the number of people contacting him. On the Sunday following his first workshop session, he had shared with the congregation what he was doing.

Once people knew he was learning about issues that concerned them, they came to him in great numbers.

Pastoral Responses

One of the keys to developing a pastoral ministry with persons who have suffered abuse is to make it known to one's congregation that one is knowledgeable about such issues. Once members of a congregation become aware of a pastor's sensitivity, concern, and knowledge, they will be anxious to share their struggles and seek assistance.

An important way to begin this process is for pastors to let their congregations know that they recognize the prevalence of family violence, that they are concerned about those who have experienced it, and that it is okay to talk about the feelings, frustrations, and spiritual problems that confront them as a result of their abusive experience. This can be done in a variety of ways. Pastors can acknowledge national observances such as Child Abuse Prevention month, Victims' Rights Week, and commemorations of the victims of family violence. This can be done by newsletter announcements, displays on bulletin boards, and sermons on these topics, or at least by references to family violence within sermons on these occasions. Pastors can make information available about shelters and treatment programs on their bulletin boards and in their notices. They can announce events or special films being offered in the community or on television about these issues.

Concern for family violence can also be evidenced by the way pastors approach traditional religious and secular celebrations such as Mother's Day, Father's Day, baptisms, and weddings. The illustrations used in sermons can acknowledge that not all parents are perfect, that infants being baptized need to be protected, not only in the world at large but sometimes even in their own families, and that marriages all too often result in violence.

Pastors can also open the doors to survivors of family violence by the way in which they conduct premarital counseling. They should be alert to any indication of violence in the relationship. The simple statement by a blushing bride that her fiancé "has a bad temper" should be followed up, no matter how jokingly the statement is made. Although pastors should be careful not to make assumptions and jump to conclusions, such statements should not be ignored. Even if it is not an unconscious request for help, such a statement can provide the occasion for gentle but firm education about the importance of identifying and managing disagreements and stresses in a relationship and the inappropriateness of physical violence. Couples also need to be aware of the ease with which violence can escalate in a relationship. The process that begins with a slap can all too easily graduate into severe blows. One of the more pernicious myths about the battering of women is that it will stop "when we get married." Lenore Walker's research (1979:30) indicates that such is not the case; the violence actually escalates.

Although we do not want to distress or frighten couples in the glow of young love, the reality and frequency of family violence is too disturbing to ignore. Such discussions during premarital counseling may provide the impetus for either partner to seek assistance at a later time, if violence should occur. They will at least have heard that violence is not a natural part of marriage and that there are resources for help.

The same sensitivity to hints of violence should be part of all pastoral counseling. All too often women and children (the most frequent victims) are afraid to talk about their experience of violence or do not know how to face the issues. They will often hint at their problems in very general terms, such as the aforementioned "bad temper," hoping that their pastor or rabbi will read between the lines of such generalizations.

If pastors and rabbis are going to be available to the victims and survivors in their congregations—as well as those persons who may someday join those ranks—in any of the ways that have been suggested, they must develop three fundamentals. First, they need a basic knowledge about family violence, the dynamics and belief structures which perpetuate it, and the long-term problems that result; second, they should collect information about the kinds of services available to victims and survivors; and, third, they must enhance their personal sympathy and sensitivity about the psychological and theological issues related to family violence.

This book provides basic knowledge about family violence and its impact on the personal and spiritual growth of those who experience it. Other sources are available, and many more are being developed. This issue is receiving increasing attention from publishers, both religious and secular.

However, pastors must also have information about local resources. The kinds of resources vary widely from place to place. Pastors need to consult their local telephone directories to identify the human services available and where they are located, or at least the methods for contacting them.

Pastors should make personal contacts with the staffs of these agencies and shelters and attend the training workshops and information sessions they offer. Such direct contact will provide a feel for the services available and the personnel involved. Armed with this information, pastors will be able to speak with greater confidence to survivors and victims about the kinds of help available and to personalize any referrals that must be made.

Most agencies are willing and anxious to meet with clergy because they recognize that they are often the first point of contact for both victims and perpetrators and that they can be an important support for survivors struggling to make changes in their lives. They are also anxious to meet knowledgeable and sensitive pastors and rabbis with whom they can consult and to whom they can refer persons with religious questions.

The third item, that of developing appropriate sympathy and sensitivity for these issues, is the most difficult. To accomplish this, pastors must examine their own assumptions and preconceptions about family violence. They must evaluate their philosophical and theological approach to these issues. Reflections in previous chapters of this book should provide food for thought about one's assumptions and preconceptions.

However, such a reflective process must also include an assessment of one's own life. Many of our perspectives and responses are determined by the kind of family in which we were raised and by the kind of family in which we presently live. The issues and concerns brought by survivors of family violence can challenge our own ways of relating to members of our families, the power relationships within our families, and the methods we use in disciplining our children. Such an examination can be disconcerting and anxiety-producing, but it can also contribute to personal growth.

Male pastors must also recognize that their gender can have a significant impact on their relationship to survivors of family violence. A male pastor must recognize that he is going to be viewed with great suspicion and apprehension by any woman or child who has been abused by a man. He will have to approach such persons with great gentleness and accept their fear and distrust as a natural result of their experience. He will have to be patient and supportive, allowing them adequate time and opportunity to share their stories.

A male pastor must also develop an understanding of feminism and feminist theology if he hopes to empower women who have previously felt helpless in their relationships. He needs to be aware of his own inevitable sexism as well as of the patriarchal advantages he experiences, even unconsciously.

No matter how vigorously we males may struggle against sexism in our society, we still retain vestiges of it and we certainly experience the advantages provided by it. A woman who has experienced violence at the hands of a domineering and chauvinist man is going to be particularly sensitive to even the most inadvertent expressions of sexism. We must be open enough about these issues and committed enough in our search for a nonsexist society that we can allow these women to vent their frustration and anger in our presence—and support them in the process.

That last statement also suggests another area where pastors must confront their feelings and preconceptions about anger: attitudes toward and comfort with expressions of anger. It is important for survivors of family violence to express their justifiable anger. The responses of trusted advisers can have a profound impact on the ability of individuals to express difficult emotions. Therefore, pastors must be comfortable enough with expressions of anger that they can allow persons to vent their feelings without being threatened. Pastors should not feel compelled to tell survivors that "everything will be all right" and "it is not necessary to be so angry" and they should try to "forgive and forget." The discussions of the religious conflicts around anger in chapter 6 and the counseling issues in chapter 9 should provide material for reflection on this matter.

Pastors must also be comfortable enough with their sexuality to allow victims of sexual violence to discuss their experiences, in as much detail as they need to, without becoming nervous and uncomfortable or shutting them off. A negative response by the pastor revictimizes survivors; they will feel it is wrong to discuss such matters, right at the time when they most need to examine and resolve them.

Pastors must also be clear about their feelings toward violence and physical discipline. Is physical discipline all right? Is the severity of the discipline the only question to be asked? Pastors who approve of physical discipline may too easily dismiss a survivor's description of this experience. Such dismissal is, once again, a form of revictimization.

Awareness of and sensitivity to the issues of family violence may therefore challenge pastors to examine some critical assumptions in their own lives. The problems created by family violence provide many new opportunities and challenges for ministry and pastoral care. They can also provide occasions of personal growth for clergy. They will discover new dimensions in the lives of their parishioners and new challenges for their ministry.

Congregational Responses

Finding new ministries and additional pastoral responsibilities are probably not top priorities for most overworked pastors.

However, the needs of survivors of family violence are real and their numbers are increasing. Not all these needs for pastoral care can or should be met personally by the pastor.

Pastors may find parishioners who are already involved in family violence programs as board members, staff, or volunteers or as professional counselors dealing extensively with this issue. Such persons can provide resources for planning and referral. Many of them may be willing to come together as a consulting, support, or referral group within the congregation to focus on the needs of survivors of family violence.

Other congregations, especially small or rural ones, may lack the people or skills to develop internal programs to serve survivors. In such cases, as well as in large congregations, pastors can provide services by making space available for programs sponsored by family violence prevention agencies. Such agencies are often looking for space to conduct support groups for battered wives or survivors of child abuse or incest. They need space to provide training programs for their own volunteers. Most agencies will be glad to have their groups or programs announced at the parish that is providing space. In this way parishes can indicate their concern and parishioners needing assistance can learn about services and have their needs met without the pastor having personally to provide the service.

Another way to deal with issues of concern to survivors of family violence is to provide workshops and adult education programs on the topic for the congregation. Such programs provide important information for the congregation in general as well as for survivors. That information may be a significant contribution toward the resolution of the issues faced by survivors. Such programs would also sensitize the broader range of members in the congregation to the needs of the survivors among them. The discussions that might occur after such programs, either in the group or privately with the presenter, can provide survivors with opportunities to share their experiences and thus break their isolation. Such responses will make the congregation an environment that is supportive to survivors. In this way, also, the needs within a congregation can be met without the pastor's having to be the sole source of counsel.

Not all programs and services need to be explicitly focused on family violence to provide for the needs of survivors. We have already discussed the ways pastors can be sensitive to these issues in premarital and marriage counseling. Congregation-wide programs already in place need only take into consideration the real possibility of violence. And other programs can be instituted or adapted to take family violence into account.

Grief support groups are commonly offered within congregations. Most survivors of family violence are confronted with grief. A battered wife escaping a violent husband will, along with her relief and newfound freedom, grieve for the relationship that has been lost. If her sorrow is not resolved she may return to the abusive relationship. Grown-up abused children experience grief as they recognize what they were deprived of by their families. For such survivors, grief support groups can provide significant assistance for their continuing survival.

Another program congregations could offer would be preparenting or parenting classes. Raising children is a difficult task. Too few programs exist to prepare or to assist parents for this difficult and demanding calling. Churches and synagogues are natural places for this task because of their concern for family values. Such courses can focus on the processes of child development and the issues of discipline related to each stage of development. Nonviolent and nurturing ways to accomplish such discipline would be examined, as well as training in conflict resolution skills and in constructive and nonviolent ways to express anger. Such courses could also discuss the kinds of personal development and support parents need for themselves. If parents are going to raise children effectively, they need a high level of self-esteem, confidence, and self-control. They also need decision-making and communication skills as well as guidance on how to develop support communities that can provide for the care and feeding of their own emotional needs.

Resources, human as well as curricular, for such programs can be found in the child-life courses presently offered in many high schools. Kathleen and James McGinnis's book *Parenting for Peace and Justice* provides excellent study materials. The Bellflower Center for Prevention of Child Abuse in Cleveland has developed a fifteen-week "nurturing program" to help families learn to use positive discipline techniques, recognize and express feelings, give and take praise, feel comfortable with touching, manage family stress, and play together and enjoy each other's company. Such a program could be enriching for any family. Skilled adult education personnel can develop specialized programs or be trained to conduct those developed by others.

Churches and synagogues can also provide valuable services by offering courses and workshops on some of the specific topics within the programs listed above. There are few church members who cannot improve their communication and problem-solving skills or strengthen their self-esteem and confidence. Such programs can provide important services to survivors who do not wish to identify themselves as such.

Such programs will send a clear message to members of the congregation that violence within families is not acceptable and that help can be found. This congregation does not merely stand in judgment but offers itself and its resources to support persons who are seeking to end abuse in all forms. It provides support and education services that offer alternatives to violence and enable persons to develop fuller, more enriched family lives—family life in abundance.

Corporate worship services can also be an important part of a survivor's spiritual growth. Specifically designed worship services can be helpful for survivors as well as for the nonabused members with whom they join. Properly designed, such services can stir victims to become survivors and strengthen survivors in their resolve to promote their spiritual growth.

Those so blessed as to never have experienced violence can be confronted with the reality of unfairness and cruelty in our world and our families and be inspired to reach out in concern, caring, and love. The nonabused can challenge the sin of silence that surrounds family violence. They can repent for their complicity through ignorance or lack of indignation. Victims, survivors, and nonabused alike can be moved to the forgiveness that can effect a true conversion of society, a radical change in the life-styles that contribute to and condone the violent nature of our society.

A Service of Commitment to Survivors of Family Violence

The following Order of Service was designed by an ecumenical group in Cleveland to highlight the issue of family violence and break the silence that surrounds it. It is offered as an example of the kind of service that can be conducted.

Bringing the Secret to Light

Call to Worship

First Reading   Ephesians 5:11–17
     We are called to expose the secret.

Silent Reflection

Communal Confession

   God of Mercy, we confess that we are humbled and frightened by the anger, hatred, and violence we know is rampant in our society and in the world, and which we sometimes feel within ourselves. We acknowledge our blindness to the secret of violence locked within our private lives.

We confess our deafness to the voices of pain that need to be heard out of the loud silence. We feel our numbness to the suffering of both the victims and perpetrators of violence, numbering among them ourselves.

God of Forgiveness, we come before you from the pseudo-sanctity of the house that harbors hidden violence. We confess that this is where we all reside. We have been participants by our complacency when we would be compassionate; by being judgmental when we would be empathic; by thinking ourselves outside the family of violence when we would be spiritual kin. Hear now, our silent personal confession.

Hymn   "By the Babylonian Rivers"

Assurance of Pardon

Second Reading   Luke 13:10–13
Our hope lies in the sign of a woman whose life was unbent by the healing power of God.

Silent Reflection

Statement of Belief and Commitment
We believe in God the Creator,
who created all things and all persons as good,
who entrusted the care of all things and all persons to other persons so that we might preserve, maintain, and foster that goodness.

We acknowledge that we humans have not always been faithful to that trust.
We have turned God's original blessing into a source of original sin.
We have failed to nurture God's goodness and have created violence even in our families.

Despite our failure,
we continue to believe in the goodness of God's creation.

We believe in Jesus the Christ, our redeemer and healer,
who lived among us in a human family,
who proclaimed and lived the true love which brings all persons to their fullness,
who gave himself into the violence of the cross so that all violence and death could be overcome by his resurrection.

We believe in the Spirit, the Sanctifier,
who enlivens us with the spirit of truth and love,

who challenges us with the spirit of wisdom and justice to
heal all division, remove all violence, and reaffirm all
goodness
that families may be made one,
persons may be made whole, and all people may come to
the fullness of peace through a community of believers
committed to acknowledging family violence among us,
removing its causes, and healing its results.

Yes, we believe, we believe that
    God has created goodness,
    Jesus has bought healing,
    The Spirit proclaims peace
    for all families.
                                    Amen.

Prayer of Intercession
    Sisters and brothers, we acknowledge that violence exists in
    families in our land, and we commit ourselves to exposing
    that violence and freeing those who suffer such violence from
    its crippling effects. Therefore, let us pray.

    For children who suffer pain, degradation, and rejection
    from those responsible for their care,
    Grant them safety and protection, Lord.

    For parents who suffer the anguish of their failures as
    parents,
    Grant them insight and healing, Lord.

    For women who are abused and battered by those who
    profess to love them,
    Grant them strength and courage, Lord.

    For men who batter those they love,
    **Grant them the repentance which can change their lives,
    Lord.**

    For all those who suffer violence in their families,
    Grant them love, solace, and healing, Lord.

    For all Christians and people of good will,
    **Grant them openness to and compassion for those who
    suffer family violence, Lord.**

    Lord God, God of Love and Creator of the universe, restore
    all families to your loving care. Teach them calm strength and
    patient wisdom that they may overcome arrogance and
    division as well as anger and violence, that they may resolve

conflicts without violence, and nurture one another in the spirit of love and peace proclaimed by Jesus our Lord. **Amen.**

Charge and Benediction

9

Binding Up the Wounds: Considerations for the Pastoral Counselor

Many of the needs of survivors can be met by sensitive and caring responses from clergy who are aware of their needs and by adult education programs that are designed with an eye to these needs. However, not all psychotherapeutic needs can be met in this way. Survivors confront many complex issues about their identity and self-image, about their perception of the world and the people around them, and about their ability to manage their emotions. Most survivors can be effectively treated through standard counseling procedures, as long as the counselor is sensitive to the dynamics of abuse and the processes of treatment appropriate for helping survivors of abuse. However, the problems of some survivors (those with multiple personalities and severe dissociation problems, for example) require treatment from persons with specialized therapy skills; the problems confronted in the treatment of abusers demand even more specialized skills and understanding.

This chapter will only address some issues in which trained pastoral counselors can be of help to survivors. We will also look at the role of groups in providing both support and therapy.

Remembering in Order to Recover

Many times Grown-Up Abused Children group members have reported that former counselors have told them, "Don't tell me about the abuse you've experienced. I don't want to talk about it. It happened ten years ago. Forget it and go on." These counselors deny the relevance of past abuse to present problems and refuse to discuss it, even though this issue is the survivor's single most pressing concern.

At other times prospective members of a group say that the reason they want to join the group is so they can "learn how to forget" their past abusive experience. I tell these persons that if they are committed to that agenda they have come to the wrong place. I explain that my goal in the group is to help them remember the past, sometimes even specific incidents, in great detail. It is necessary to recall those incidents in order to see their relationships to present behaviors and problems. Furthermore, survivors are never really going to forget what happened, no matter how hard they try. These events are part of their lives; there is no way to erase them, and it is counterproductive to try. It takes great amounts of psychic energy to repress anger and block such memories. And, in fact, many survivors report great and welcome increases in personal energy levels when past repressed feelings and incidents are allowed to surface and be remembered.

Trying to forget is also counterproductive because it often results in merely disguising the issue. Even if the person, at some level, successfully blocks the memories—and some people have successfully blocked whole periods of their lives—only the focus of the problem is changed. Their concerns move from anger about abuse to anxiety about aquariums, from fear of or anger at their fathers or abusive husbands to distrust of all men. They may successfully block a bad memory, but they create other problems for themselves in the process.

On the other hand, the purpose of the Grown-Up Abused Children program is not to dwell on the past or exchange horror stories. The starting point of any discussion is a problem someone is encountering now. However, many of the persistent problems of the present have their origin in past abusive experiences. Excessive anxiety, raging fears, and uncontrollable behaviors are frequently learned responses to a violent past. The group will help such individuals identify the experiences of the past that have connections with or similarities to their present difficulties.

These connections are not always immediately clear. Often group members have come into a meeting visibly upset. When asked to share what is bothering them, they say, "It is not appropriate for this group." After being convinced to at least discuss it with the group and let the members determine whether the material is appropriate, they frequently discover that their present problem—be it with a boyfriend, husband, children, friends, or schoolwork—has a connection to their past experience. Part of the reason for the difficulty, or part of the reason they are unable to resolve a fairly minor dilemma, stems from the similarity of this event to past events or to anxieties they have carried over from earlier days. Seeing the connections facilitates resolution of the problem.

When past incidents that have connections to the present are identified, they may have to be examined in great detail to determine which aspects of that experience are affecting the present. Usually this process of recollection can be done in a straightforward manner. Simple discussion of past and present events can identify similarities and differences.

Other times the process becomes more complicated because the group member has blocked from memory significant details about the past experience. If such persons have only vague recollections of related past events, they may find it helpful to close their eyes and try to put themselves back into the situation, remembering as many details as possible about the room, the clothes they were wearing, exterior noises—anything that will help them relive the experience.

This can become very painful. Often in this process, such a counselee begins to recall particularly unpleasant aspects of the event. She or he may recall for the first time that sexual abuse was involved or that there were other members of family present who did not offer assistance. A counselor must be supportive at this difficult time, but it is extremely important for the survivor to deal with these painful recollections. It is often the unremembered, blocked aspects of an experience that hold the key to a survivor's present problems.

Sometimes there seems to be no recollection of past events at all. Don't force the issue and accuse the person of blocking. Such an approach simply increases anxiety, reinforces low self-esteem, and makes the process more difficult. A counselor should simply lay out the possibility, encourage the client to consider it, and leave it for the client's own reflection. Periodically the counselor may ask if the person has had any further insights on the matter, but not in such a way as to create more anxiety. If, of course, a counselor is experienced in hypnosis and a client is willing, this process can be very helpful in uncovering blocked memories.

In whatever manner the counselor decides to approach the issue, he or she must remember there is no guarantee that there is any repressed material that needs to be remembered. However, with survivors of abuse the probability that something has been repressed is very high. Whatever is uncovered must be taken seriously, because remembering can help map the road to recovery.

Dreaming Dreams to See Visions

Some people would not describe themselves as grown-up abused children because they do not recall that they were beaten, molested, or otherwise mistreated. They do not remember anything. They do not remember abuse; neither do they remember pleasant times. For many survivors (even some who realize they are such), large blocks of their lives are lost. For these people, remembering is an even more difficult process. Their only key is their subconscious.

For such persons the beginning of the recollection process is to be found in their dreams or in flashbacks and fleeting images they experience while awake. These dreams or flashbacks may contain sexual or physically violent images or explicit incidents for which they have no conscious recollection. Frequently such survivors discount these experiences as hallucinations. Therapists may also discount such images as hallucinations or Freudian fantasies.

However, these images are often the first signs of a past seeking to be recalled, forgotten experiences striving to be remembered, a traumatic incident begging to be recognized. These images are part of what psychological researchers call "intrusive recollections" of a traumatic event (see vol. 3 of the American Psychiatric Association's *Diagnostic and Statistical Manual,* or *DSM,* 1980:236)—one of the characteristic symptoms of post-traumatic stress disorder (PTSD).

PTSD is a clinical diagnostic category which recognizes that a survivor of trauma may reexperience "elements of the trauma in dreams, uncontrollable and emotionally distressing intrusive images and dissociative mental states." A survivor also experiences "a loss of normal affect and emotional responsiveness, and exhibits less interest and involvement in work and interpersonal relationships" (Green 1981:3). The two characteristics may coexist in an individual or occur in cycles.

These reactions are common occurrences in persons who have experienced a "recognizable stressor that would evoke significant symptoms of distress in almost everyone" (*DSM* 1980:238). Such "stressors" can range from natural disasters (tornadoes and floods) to accidental manmade disasters (car accidents and fires) and deliberate manmade disasters (bombings, torture, military combat, and child abuse), all of which produce trauma outside normal experience.

Several factors affect the severity of a person's reaction. "The disorder is apparently more severe and longer lasting when the stressor is of human design" (*DSM* 1980:236). The severity of the response is also "dependent in large part on the nature and intensity of the individual's personal experience of a traumatic event" (Green 1981:10). "The specific meaning of the event to an individual [is also] a factor in the working through process" (ibid., p. 12).

Family violence certainly ranks high as a recognizable stressor outside of normal experience. It also contains factors that intensify the disorder. It is of human design, it is intensely personal, and most batterers have attached specific messages about their victim's personal meaning and value to the blows they inflict.

Victims of family violence also lack a key ingredient that can help them adapt to the effects of the stress and integrate the experience into a healthy perception of reality: a supportive environment. What should be their principal source of support— the family—is instead the source of their trauma. Often when the abuse is discovered, even that inadequate source of stability disintegrates. If the victim has sought aid and been rejected, the disorders caused by the severe stress are compounded.

Persons who have endured extreme stressors may experience a number of stress reactions immediately after the event, such as anxiety, inability to sleep, and nightmares. However, some people initially report no unusual reactions or have no recollection of the event. Weeks, months, or even years later they begin to reexperience the trauma. According to the American Psychiatric Association *(DSM* 1980:238), this may manifest itself through:

1. Recurrent and intrusive recollections of the event
2. Recurrent dreams of the event
3. Sudden acting or feeling as if the traumatic event were recurring, because of an association with an environmental or ideational stimulus

These persons also report new psychological symptoms, such as:

1. Hyperalertness or exaggerated startle response
2. Sleep disturbance
3. Guilt about surviving when others have not, or about behavior required for survival
4. Memory impairment or trouble concentrating
5. Avoidance of activities that arouse recollection of the traumatic event
6. Intensification of symptoms by exposure to events that symbolize or resemble the traumatic event

These are the signs that a traumatic event is striving to reassert itself. The process of denial, which may have been necessary to manage the psychic overload of an intense or outrageous experience, is beginning to break down. This kind of breakdown constitutes a sign of health. New strengths are developing that enable the person to face the trauma and work it through to an integrated view of the world and of self. Now new information can become an integral part of the survivor's personality.

In this phase of treatment the survivor not only begins to acknowledge the traumatic past but also to confront maladaptive behaviors that have been a part of his or her defense system; the use of chemicals, fantasies about or actual attempts at suicide, or the phobic avoidance of situations that bring back the trauma are no longer needed. The survivor may also experience relief from the depression and "psychic numbing" which has ruled his or her life.

Since the key to healing for sufferers from PTSD (for our purposes, survivors of family violence) is movement from denial to recognition and integration, the experience of intrusive images in the form of unexplainable dreams and flashbacks is a positive part of the process. Pastoral counselors must reassure their clients that such experiences are a natural and important part of healing. They must encourage clients to foster rather than resist these images and follow them to their natural conclusions.

The process of working with these intrusive images is the same as that for dealing with the vague and incoherent recollections that some survivors may have. The images need to be discussed in detail. The counselor must help the client focus on the pieces of information that are available and strive to reconstruct the details of the original experience.

There is a caution to be observed, however. Whenever possible, efforts to reconstruct the details should not be made alone. The survivor should attempt to reconstruct the traumatic experience only during times when a trusted friend or counselor is available. The survivor will usually need support, reassurance, and even control when going through such an experience. Part of the nature of PTSD is that reliving the trauma can be a total sense experience. All the past sights, smells, and feelings can recur. This can be painful and disorienting. The person may forget the present surroundings and act in a bizarre fashion. In addition to the problems associated with reliving the event, the survivor may become emotionally disoriented. Recalling the experience may add a whole new dimension to life, which may require a redefinition of self and the reality of the person's family and world. A supportive and understanding counselor is essential in such circumstances.

This process is not easy. It can be so painful and disconcerting that there may be many good reasons to avoid the whole thing.

Such difficulties seem to provide a good rationale for blocking the process. But flashbacks and intrusive images will keep coming until they are dealt with and resolved. What seems to be "successful" denial leads to unsuccessful conduct. Common maladaptive behaviors that help hide the reality of trauma include depression, drug abuse, suicide, and actions destructive to personal relationships—the many behaviors we have discussed.

Most survivors have their own vision of what they want their lives to be and what it means to be whole, to experience caring family relationships, to live at peace. As contradictory as it may seem, their disturbing dreams and unwanted images are an important step toward attaining that vision. By reliving the pain they relieve their anxieties, resolve their conflicts, and establish loving relationships. It is a pastoral counselor's unpleasant but rewarding task to prod them into pain so they can attain vision.

The Present Is Not the Past

One of the problems experienced by survivors is that they are not able to separate past traumatic events from present experience. They experience flashbacks of their past trauma in such a vivid manner that it is difficult to distinguish it from present reality.

In such cases of post-traumatic stress the flashbacks can be so strong that there is complete disassociation from the present. The survivor perceives the people he or she is dealing with in the present as if they are people out of the past: for example, military enemies, captors, or abusers. The survivor has had a complete shift in time and place and responds as if reliving a past situation. At such times, the person experiencing the flashback has little or no recollection of present actions or behaviors during the flashback after it has subsided.

Other persons experience flashbacks in a different way. They have a vivid recollection, but they know it is an incident out of the past. They do not have any disassociation with persons, places, or times. It is similar to having a daydream in the middle of a boring class. You know you are still in class, but you are able to escape for a few moments to a different time and place.

Survivors of family violence can experience either of these kinds of flashbacks. In both instances the role of the counselor is to help the survivors manage their experiences and understand and assimilate the content of the flashback. If the survivor is completely disassociating, the counselor must help the person identify the factors that triggered the flashbacks. This could involve talking about events that immediately preceded the experience and trying to understand what element of sight, touch, smell, or sound may have reminded the person of the past and jarred her or him back into the previously traumatic experience.

It is critical that survivors learn to identify the circumstances that trigger flashbacks so they can appreciate the meaning of the flashback for their present lives and control them in the future. The counselor must also help them recall their actions during the flashback so they can talk about the content of the experience. In this way they will be able to share that experience with others, understand it better, and assimilate its meaning for their lives.

In those flashback experiences in which there is no disassociation, it is also important to identify the triggers, so the survivors can understand what factors in their lives are closely associated with their abusive pasts. This can enable them to have greater control over not only the flashbacks but also the ways in which the past abuse impacts on present behavior. They need to share past experiences with others in order to realize that others have them also and to integrate the experiences into their present lives.

Survivors often have another kind of problem distinguishing their past experiences from their present life. In many situations they may be in touch with reality, fully aware of the present, and yet their experience is loaded with baggage from the past. Unwittingly, they react in the present the same way that they would have reacted to a similar person or situation in the past.

What is happening is similar to transference in a therapeutic situation. However, the transference is not to a therapist but to various persons or circumstances that remind them of their past. The survivors impose on present persons and situations the feelings, attitudes, and attributes that belong to significant persons or events of the past and act accordingly. As in classic transference, this involves unconscious fantasies and new versions of old conflicts based on perceptions of some real aspects of the present which are similar to events of the past. The survivor does not recognize anything unusual happening. A particular person may make them uncomfortable or angry, but there is some "rational" explanation for these feelings. It is only after the "reasons" have been proven inadequate that they begin to recognize the ways in which this person or situation reminds them of the past. "She wears her hair just like my mother." "He uses the same words and mannerisms as my father; I know he is going to get angry with me."

Such responses can be particularly devastating for survivors of incest. For them, the transference process occurs in the most intimate circumstances and interferes with loving relations.

"Everything was fine until he touched me that way." "Everything was fine until he said the same words my father used to say."

In many cases survivors do not recognize the triggers of the transference process. In such cases the counselor must help them analyze the details of their experience and ascertain the similarities with the past in order to make the proper identifications. When the connections are known, the counselor can proceed directly to developing appropriate interpretations of the present so that it can be distinguished from the past. In some cases the connections are so strong that the best way for the survivor to manage present circumstances is to avoid those situations that trigger transference and flashbacks.

In all these matters, counselors need to be patient and pay great attention to detail in order to identify the specific elements that create problems for their counselees. Only through this attention to detail can the proper connections be made and the insights gained that enable survivors to be aware of their problems, resolve their internal conflicts, and make changes that will enhance their lives.

Be Angry

Carol had been a member of a Grown-Up Abused Children group for almost two years. She had made great progress. However, one problem persisted. Every time the topic of anger came up or someone in the group expressed anger in any way, she would push her chair away from the circle into a corner and cringe in fear, curled up in an almost fetal position in her chair. Each time this happened the group would ask her why she did it, why she was so afraid. Her response was that when people got angry she was afraid they were going to hit her. The group reassured her that no one was angry at her, and no one was going to strike her. These reassurances had little effect.

One day her response broadened to include another element. She said, "I am afraid I am going to get angry." She could offer no explanation about why someone else's anger was going to make her angry.

At one meeting, after this had gone on for some time, when Carol again retreated to her corner and curled up in her fetal position, I pulled my chair directly in front of her. Gently, I unwrapped her arms from around herself and encouraged her to put one of her clenched fists in the palm of my hand. She did so with great reluctance. I urged her to push on it. Her response was, "I can't. I might hurt you." I assured her that it would not hurt me. She would not be striking me but only pushing against my hand. I explained that I was trying to get her to release the tension that was coiled in her body. Reluctantly and hesitantly, she began to push on my hand, pausing periodically to inquire if she was hurting me. I assured her she was not. She finally relaxed a little bit but stated that she had to stop because she was afraid to do any more. We stopped and she rejoined the group.

This process was repeated periodically over the next several weeks. I got her to the point where she would punch gently at the palm of my hand. Finally, she got more aggressive with her punches and I had to hold a chair cushion in my hand. Each time, we discussed her feelings about what she was doing, as well as the anger she was feeling and the object of that anger.

After one session Carol confided that she wished she had the courage to go into one of the porno shops a few blocks down the street. Amazed, the group members asked why she wanted to do that. Her reply was, "I understand you can buy life-size anatomically correct dolls. I would like to get one to beat on." "Would you like a male doll?" a woman in the group asked. "I'll sew one for the next meeting."

True to her word, the woman arrived at the next meeting with a life-sized stuffed doll. She had sewn a shirt to a pair of pants, added a head, and stuffed the whole arrangement with old rags and packing material. And if you unzipped the jeans, Max, as he was quickly named, was anatomically correct.

Carol's initial reaction to Max was fear. Gradually, she approached him, propped up in a chair, and punched him gently, stepping back and laughing nervously each time she did it. Soon her blows became more vigorous, and she attacked Max with vengeance. Soon he was out of the chair and on the floor and being kicked and punched repeatedly while Carol screamed obscenities. All the time she was doing this, I stood behind her with my hands gently on her shoulders, saying, "Carol, remember who this is, remember who you are really angry at." Eventually Carol's anger subsided and she collapsed in exhaustion. She surveyed the group and asked if everyone was all right. They assured her they were fine and that what she had done was good.

Carol began to talk, in greater detail than ever before, about the abuse her father had heaped upon her and the anger that she always felt but was afraid to express. Her anger had reached such proportions she was afraid that she would hurt someone if she ever let it out. This was the first time she had ever allowed such feelings to surface.

"What do I do now?" she asked, "I feel relieved, but I am also afraid that I am going to get angry again. I won't have Max to beat on and I may hurt someone." I assured her that she would indeed feel angry again and that she would have to be careful to control it around other people. When she was alone, she might try beating on pillows or overstuffed chairs. We would need to have many more discussions in the future to help her learn to manage her anger and express it appropriately.

Carol's anger was a topic of discussion at each of the meetings over the next several weeks. In the beginning, she acknowledged that she felt angry on many occasions, "almost constantly." Gradually, the frequency of the emotion diminished and she was able to put her feelings in perspective. She was able to sort out what things were appropriately making her angry and which events were simply reminding her of her father's abuse in the past. She developed additional methods for expressing her anger, including calm conversation with people who might have offended her. She developed a whole new repertoire of interpersonal skills.

Carol's story is one of the more dramatic examples of a grown-up abused child getting in touch with and wanting to express her anger. It exemplifies some of the problems that survivors of abuse have with anger. They are afraid of other people's anger, they get confused, anxious, and afraid about their own anger, and they are afraid that their own emotions will overwhelm them. They also may have moral or religious conflicts about allowing themselves to feel angry.

Survivors of abuse are not the only people who have difficulty dealing with anger. Most people feel uncomfortable with it. Even counselors can be uncomfortable with other people's expressions of anger. I must confess to no little anxiety when Carol began to rant and rave at Max. It is not easy to sit quietly while someone seems to throw a temper tantrum. It is not easy to be supportive if some of the rage is inappropriately directed at you.

A counselor can also have appropriate reservations about being able to control such persons so they do not hurt themselves or others. Counselors are often confronted with the question of whether a person's anger is adequately in control so that they will not hurt someone in a fit of rage outside the counseling setting. All these questions can provide anxious moments.

On a purely theoretical level, the question must be asked about the role of anger and its expression in good mental health. Is it an appropriate emotion? Should it be repressed and controlled, or should it be vented and expressed with great energy and conviction?

Few people would deny that anger is a part of everyone's life (although I have had grown-up abused children say that they have never been angry), but is it more effective to keep it to yourself or express it to the world around you? Will you feel better or worse after you express your anger? We have all probably had occasions when we felt better and others when we felt worse.

For purposes of this discussion, let me define anger as an emotional response to insult or injury and the communication of those feelings. The emotional response may have attendant physiological reactions, and there are many different ways that these feelings can be communicated. The feelings can be communicated to the source of injury or to others who will share the offended person's reaction. All three elements of this definition are interrelated, but the emotional response and the communication of feelings are the most closely related.

What constitutes an insult or injury can vary greatly from person to person and within cultures and families. In some ethnic groups, loud arguments are the order of the day. If members of the family have not disagreed vigorously about some issue during a family reunion, it has not been a successful event. In other families, such discussions would be cause for insult, and the family members would never speak to each other again.

Survivors of abuse may have distorted images of what constitutes an insult or injury. Some are too sensitive in certain situations. Statements intended to be helpful are seen as put-downs, gestures intended to comfort are perceived as threats. Such persons need help to reinterpret such experiences in their lives.

Simply telling them "You should not be so sensitive" is not helpful. They need to see why their behaviors are out of the ordinary, to determine what would be appropriate, and to see that the situations they are reacting to are in a different social context from what they experienced in their families. What was an insult in their families is not necessarily so in other situations. A threatening gesture in their family may be a sign of friendship for other people.

Other survivors may be totally insensitive to insult or injury. They accept any ridicule or put-down as treatment they deserve. They see no reason to be angry, no matter what injustice is perpetrated on them; such acts are merely a confirmation of their worthlessness. To encourage these persons to be angry is a waste of time at this stage in their development. They must first be helped to enhance their self-esteem. Then they will be able to develop a sense of insult and injury.

When an injury is perceived, most people experience physiological reactions—muscle tension, clenched fists, flushed cheeks, sweaty palms. Research indicates that anger induces increased pulse rate and higher blood pressure. Such reactions are a natural part of the human response to injury. Even survivors who deny they ever feel angry do so through clenched teeth. For them, the emotion of anger is too dangerous. If they responded with anger when they were abused, it caused greater violence. Instead of anger's being a method for regaining control over their lives, it resulted in losing even more control. For them, anger was also mixed with fear, anxiety, and frustration. Because the latter emotions predominated, they learned it was safer to repress and block their feelings. For them, denial was the best policy.

But is it the best policy? Contemporary research indicates that the repression of anger increases the physiological reactions. Repression contributes to high blood pressure and may result in damage to one's heart. A psychological adage maintains that depression is anger turned inward. Survivors of abuse frequently suffer from severe depression. Such evidence suggests that denial of anger is not a recommended course of action.

However, the survivor who has learned to repress feelings of anger does not realize there is anything to communicate. How does one get from denial to communication? A pastoral counselor can be helpful in this process by observing the body language of the survivor—the tension, the flushed face, the clenched fists. Without ever using the word "anger," the counselor can ask the survivor, "When such a thing happens, or when you recall what your parents did to you, how does your body feel? Do you feel tense in your shoulders, butterflies in your stomach, or hot all over? What does that physical feeling make you want to do?" The counselor can ask what the survivor would like to do to relieve those symptoms, if she or he were able to do anything at all.

This kind of discussion does not invoke the emotionally laden word "anger." Nevertheless, it helps survivors identify their physiological reactions to injury or insult. After they are able to identify the reactions, they can connect them to the emotion and realize that they do indeed feel angry.

Then the counselor must reassure clients that anger is an appropriate reaction, that he or she would feel angry in a similar situation, and that there are various ways to deal with and express anger.

What are those appropriate ways to express anger? Many people, and not only those who have suffered family violence, feel that anger is a useless and even destructive emotion, better kept to oneself. Such people say it doesn't do any good to express anger; it often makes matters worse. Is there a way to express anger without making things worse?

The most popularly acclaimed method for expressing anger today is ventilation—letting it all hang out, getting things off your chest, yelling and screaming. This is touted as a cure for high blood pressure and as a means to better mental health. It certainly was what Carol did, and it seemed to help her.

For persons who have denied anger for many years, ventilation can be an effective way to get in touch with the emotion. It helps them learn what anger feels like and understand its process. They also learn not to fear it. They discover that, even in the throes of anger, they still have a level of control and can regain complete control. If this ventilation is done in a controlled environment, one where the survivor and others around them are protected and safe, ventilation can be a productive process. Particularly if there are people present who can help the survivor reflect on past experience and be clear about whom the anger is directed against and how the process of anger works, ventilation can become a fruitful learning experience.

But is ventilation the best way to react? Some abuse survivors are abusers of others. They do not need to learn how to express anger. They do so violently on many occasions. Suzanne K. Steinmetz in her book *The Cycle of Violence* (1977:24) found that the violent expression of anger (its ventilation) within families does not relieve tension and help the families deal with anger more creatively. It increases violence and teaches children that such behavior is acceptable. Her data are certainly not a strong endorsement of the ventilation-as-catharsis theory of anger.

Persons who work with abusive males also maintain that for such men the violent expression of anger is addictive. The physiological reactions associated with anger and its violent expression produce a high they find exhilarating. Such persons do not need to learn how to express their anger, they must learn to control it. The first task of a counselor is to stop the violence.

However, some people are violent even as they repress their anger. Some survivors, who were not normally violent or angry, report having committed acts of violence without experiencing anger in the process. They felt no emotions at all. It was almost as if they watched themselves perform the violent act. Some abusers also report having had no feelings during a battering episode. Their violence had no emotional content. Even though they were violent, they had successfully repressed their anger.

Such persons need to connect their anger with their violence. Once they recognize that they are angry, and identify the physiological responses that precede the violence, they can control it. They must learn that there are other ways to express what they are feeling. Such persons may also have to ventilate their anger in controlled environments, but this is not learning to yell for the sake of yelling; it is learning to recognize anger so that the emotions connected to insult or injury can be properly expressed. Survivors of abuse need first to recognize their emotions; then they can examine various ways to express them. Violence is certainly not appropriate, and yelling and screaming are certainly not the only alternatives. As Carol Tavris says (1982:44), "Anger means that something in your life is wrong." Once that fact is recognized, a person can begin to change what is wrong. Then, anger can be used constructively.

One way some grown-up abused children want to use their anger is to confront their parents about what they did to them. This is a task that must be approached cautiously. The grown-up abused child must be clear about what he or she hopes to accomplish: an apology? some change in the parent's behavior? That has proven to be unlikely. In most cases of people who were abused years ago, the parents will deny their charges or say they are blowing things out of proportion. If that is a survivor's sole reason for undertaking the confrontation, it is probably better not to try.

For those who feel that, even without an apology, they would feel better for having said their piece, this can be constructive. It doesn't always have to be done directly to the parents. Often, people have role-played conversations with their parents and decided that they did not need to speak to them directly. They found it helpful to have communicated their feelings and vocalized what was important to them. This helped them pinpoint exactly what was of concern to them. "It was not that he hit me that was important, but what he said when he did it," or, "What really upsets me is that my mother did not stop it."

This communication of feelings, even in a soft, modulated voice, can provide the catharsis necessary for grown-up abused children to stop internalizing the negative messages they received so long ago. Finally, these messages have been placed outside, so these persons can see they are not a real part of who they are. They then realize that what is wrong with life is not in themselves but in outside persons and forces which they can choose to reject. For such people, anger is the beginning of their rejection of those false and negative messages.

The Healing Touch

Many survivors have problems with touching and being touched. This is understandable, since their past experience was frequently negative. All too often, when their parents or spouses touched them it was violent, sexual, or totally unpredictable. Many times they experienced no physical contact at all. As a result, these persons developed an aversion to physical contact or inappropriate responses to it. They became clinging and overly demanding or they misinterpreted any touch as a sexual overture.

Such responses can produce problems. Even in our western nondemonstrative society, physical contact is common. People do reach out in friendship, caring, and comfort. Survivors give the wrong message if they flinch or recoil in terror or respond with great craving or sexual innuendo to every physical contact. Such responses make it difficult for them to function effectively. They turn away friends or frighten them because they are too demanding. They may unintentionally encourage a suitor.

On the other hand, they may live in constant anxiety or confusion. Many constantly fear that someone will touch them. Others are anxious to have physical contact, even as they fear the experience.

Can a pastoral counselor play a role in resolving this problem for survivors? Physical contact between counselors and clients is a topic of much controversy. Certainly any form of abusive or sexual contact is wrong. Violent and inappropriate touch was the major cause of the problems of survivors. However, touch is one of the five senses and is an important form of communication. Somehow, survivors must learn what is appropriate. They need to reestablish normal caring contact with others. They need to learn that touch can be healing.

Assuming that a counselor can, and even should, have some physical contact with a client who is a survivor, what form should it take? How does one assure that it is healing? The answer is, It all depends. It depends on the counselor, on the forms of abuse suffered, on how recently it was experienced, and on where the survivor is in the recovery process.

It depends on the counselor, because he or she must be clear about physical contact and what to consider appropriate. The person who feels awkward in touching others, or is unclear about the sexual connotations of such contact, had best avoid it. And the person who is not clear about his or her own feelings about the client should also avoid physical contact. As has been said before, survivors are very sensitive to the moods and feelings of others. They have developed a keen sixth sense about such responses to them. If the counselor is unclear or uncomfortable, the survivor will recognize that and become frightened, confused, or even seductive, depending on the abuse experienced and the level of recovery.

If the survivor experienced sexual abuse, he or she may fear that any physical contact is going to result in sexual imposition. If the sexual abuse was recent, and especially if it was violent, even a comforting hand on a shoulder may be terrifying. It may trigger flashbacks that set back the process of recovery. Such an action, despite its good intentions, may undermine trust in the counselor and destroy the possibility of future communication.

In such cases, all forms of physical contact (even a parting pat on the back) should be avoided. This is particularly true if the counselor is male and the client is female. The counselor should even avoid any sudden movements that may appear to be reaching toward the client. She has suffered a severe trauma. She needs time and space to recover.

If the sexual abuse occurred some time ago, that same comforting hand on the shoulder can still be frightening. The reactions may not be as drastic, but flashbacks can still occur. The survivor may be ambivalent about physical contact—anxious for it but frightened too. In such cases the counselor must approach the issue cautiously, discussing it with the survivor, asking how it feels to be touched in any way, and explaining that such contact is normal and healthy but that the survivor may be uncomfortable with it. The counselor should encourage the client to overcome fear and move gently in that direction by suggesting nonthreatening kinds of contact like a passing pat on the shoulder—that can be tried. However, the counselor must always respect the client's feelings and follow the client's lead.

One group member was deathly afraid of being touched. Susan made it clear at the beginning of the group's life that no one was to touch her—not even a parting pat on the back—without her permission. Occasionally, she tried to deal with her fear by having various group members hold her hand or give her a quick hug. At the conclusion of the group's final session, Susan announced that she was not leaving until everyone had given her a *big* hug. The group gladly complied. Susan approached each person with great trepidation, but she did return each hug heartily. As the group applauded, Susan beamed. She had crossed an important barrier.

Some survivors of sexual abuse have another reaction to physical contact. Rather than fearing it, they crave it and strive to create opportunities for as much contact as possible. For these people, sexual abuse was usually not violent and may have been their only experience of caring. They see any form of touch as a way to gain acceptance. They become clinging and overtly sexual in their responses to the slightest physical contact. For them, a comforting hand on the shoulder is a sexual advance. In many cases they are more than willing to respond to the imagined advance and may become hostile if it is not carried through as they perceive it should. They feel rejected because a friendly gesture has not resulted in sexual intimacy.

A pastoral counselor must be very cautious in working with such clients—in self-protection. He or she must maintain distance and avoid all forms of physical contact. The setting for the counseling appointment must be as public as possible. A group is a good setting for dealing with such persons.

After assuring his or her integrity, the counselor must help the survivor understand that certain responses to physical contact are inappropriate. He must also help the client understand the source of these reactions, so they can be changed. He must explain the basic principles of male/female interactions and point out that, contrary to earlier experience at home, care and affection can be expressed in many ways other than sexual.

If the survivor suffered physical abuse, an extended hand may be perceived as a threatening hand. Such a person was usually touched only in violence. The pastoral counselor must help the survivor develop a new understanding and experience of physical contact. He or she must explain to the survivor that a touch can be a stroke or a caress; it can be soothing as well as comforting. If the counselor wants to touch the survivor, he or she should say what is going to happen, make it clear that the survivor can stop it at any time, and should move slowly when initiating the contact.

For clients who are survivors of neglect, this fear of touching or being touched is a fear of the unknown. When someone moves to touch them, they do not know what to expect or how to react. They may react either with fear or with undue eagerness. Once again, the counselor must educate such survivors about the role of human contact in communicating friendship, affection, and intimacy, and point out that different kinds of contact have different meanings in various situations. Survivors need to learn these fundamentals of physical communication so they do not convey a message they do not intend.

Ray Helfer (1984:84) recognizes the problems survivors have with touch. "Many adults find touching to be most frightening. Others have avoided it for so many years that they fail to realize this sense is not available to them." He proceeds to devote six pages of his book to a progression of exercises that can help persons learn or relearn how to use their sense of touch. His exercises begin with a survivor stroking a piece of fur or soft cloth and learning what that feels like. Then he suggests petting a dog or cat and caressing a child, all the time paying close attention to one's feelings. Finally, the survivor asks a trusted friend (this might be one's counselor) if they can exchange a pat on the back and ultimately a hug.

This series of exercises indicates the complexity of teaching a survivor how to revive and delight in the sense of touch.

Although a pastoral counselor cannot teach survivors the joys of the full range of physical contact—serious ethical principles would be violated—he or she can help survivors overcome their initial fear and uncertainty and understand the different forms and roles of human contact. In this way, touching and being touched can become a healing part of the survivor's human experience.

Gathering Two or Three . . .

We have been discussing ways a pastoral counselor can help survivors resolve their problems through one-to-one counseling. However, one of the major problems encountered by persons who suffered family violence is a sense of isolation. Loneliness and a sense of separation compound every problem encountered by survivors of abuse. An important form of the treatment a pastoral counselor can provide is group counseling.

The most important thing the Grown-Up Abused Children program does for its participants is bring them together. The opportunity to gather with others of similar backgrounds—to share stories and struggles, to understand and be understood, to be supported, challenged, and reassured—is the most healing aspect of the program.

Those involved in pastoral counseling should strongly consider developing such a group as part of the services offered. Such a group could focus exclusively on grown-up abused children, or it could include battered women or adult children of alcoholics. The behavioral dynamics for each of these groups are similar. One pastor in Cleveland formed a support group within his parish that included people who were now or had been in dysfunctional families. This group met for a number of years with great success.

Here are some of the advantages of this form of treatment for survivors. Leehan and Wilson (1985) provide greater detail in *Grown-Up Abused Children.*

The first advantage is that the group process breaks down the isolation felt by survivors. They became separated from others because they did not learn communication skills in their families and they were told to keep their abuse a secret. If they did risk telling someone, they were frequently not believed or they were rejected or treated strangely as a result of the revelation.

Although the conspiracy of silence around family violence has been broken by new laws, increases in services, and media attention, many survivors were raised before such breakthroughs occurred. They still cannot believe it is okay to talk about their experiences or that they will be believed. They also do not see the connections between their present problems and their past abuse. A group where such matters are expected and accepted topics of discussion can destroy this isolation.

Such a group can also break down the isolation by providing support and reassurance. For some, it may be the first truly safe environment they have experienced, since their family of origin was a place of threats, violence, chaos, and rejection. It is, of course, the responsibility of the leaders to create a structure that is supportive and consistent and to establish ground rules that provide safety and security.

If such an environment can be created, persons who have lived most of their lives in fear can gain the courage to lower their defenses and share their pain, their anguish, and their desires. They will be able to communicate with one another about what happened in the past and what they hope for in the future. In this setting they will learn the process of dialogue and discussion for the first time. They will experience the give-and-take that is a normal part of sharing ideas and concerns. The group leader may have to provide some basic instruction in communication techniques, but in such a group survivors can learn about and practice communication and social skills that have never before been available to them. Such opportunities can be powerful learning and healing experiences.

Such groups add a dimension to the counseling experience that cannot be provided in a one-to-one setting. This dimension might be called the "reality factor." The reality of family violence and its long-term effects are better communicated from one survivor to another. Books on child abuse and statistics on battered women cannot communicate the same reality as a face-to-face discussion with another battered woman or grown-up abused child. Books cannot inform another survivor of the anguish and struggle necessary to overcome the past. Statistics cannot provide the solace in similarity another tearstained face can offer.

A new member of a Grown-Up Abused Children group, a businessman self-consciously dressed in gray flannel, expressed this in a touching manner. After listening to introductions by other members, he said, "I'm ashamed to say this, but I'm glad to hear what people have been saying. I don't mean I'm happy about what happened to you or about the difficulties you are experiencing, but I can't tell you what a relief it is to know I'm not the only person this kind of thing happened to, and I'm not the only one having problems like those many of you have described. And you all seem so nice. Maybe there's some hope for me after all."

After finding solace in similarity, members can also find insight and strength through that similarity. Over and over again, I have offered what I considered profound reflections and brilliant advice to group members, only to have them ignored or rejected. A couple of weeks later another group member would offer the same suggestion (not nearly so brilliantly!), and it would be accepted with enthusiasm. Members often find advice offered by other group members much more acceptable than that offered by the leader because it comes from someone who "really understands where I'm coming from."

The same is true of pressure for growth and challenges for change. "Maybe that suggestion will work. Maybe that task can be accomplished, since it comes from someone who has the same problems I do and knows how difficult it can be." Over and over again, pressure and encouragement from other group members does more to effect change than the same efforts from the group leader. The same encouragement, suggestion, or reflection achieves new meaning, is heard in a new way, and is actually accomplished.

Acceptance of and approval for deeds done also means more when it comes from other members of the group. "That really must have been a great thing I did. My fellow group members, who share my same problems, think so, anyway."

Frequently, group members get caught by their own advice. They find themselves giving advice to others that applies to themselves or that they have previously rejected. People have literally stopped in mid-sentence and said sheepishly, "I think I should follow my own advice."

Such reality effects in a counseling setting are possible when two or three or more persons with similar backgrounds are gathered together. They can enhance the impact and healing power of the counseling experience for one another. They can help one another grow and develop at a much faster rate than similar work done independently.

Pastoral counselors should consider forming a group for the survivors they encounter in their practice. Such groups, led by counselors with spiritual as well as psychological sensitivities, can make profound contributions to the growth and development of the survivors among the saints.

Conclusion

A few weeks before completing this book, my wife and I had the opportunity to spend a week with our good friends Bob and Libby Clarke, at their summer home near Rocky Mountain National Park in Colorado. We hiked in the mountains and found the vistas inspiring and breathtaking. Equally inspiring were the trees that struggle to grow near the tree line. They were twisted and bent by winds that sought to uproot them, but they persisted. They survived in a harsh environment. They are stunted and deformed, but they have a special beauty—like giant bonsai trees.

Survivors of family violence also have a special beauty. They have suffered the severest trauma humans inflict on one another. They have been twisted and bent—but they have survived. As they survived they gained great strength, acquired profound insights, and developed special skills and abilities.

Since their principal purpose was to survive, not grow, develop, or flourish, their strength may have made them rigid, their insights may have become distorted, and their lessons may have taught them some dysfunctional skills—but they have survived and they have a unique beauty.

The challenge for survivors of family violence and for those who work with them is to recognize and foster the strength and beauty in their survival and also to provide new opportunities for growth in a hospitable environment. Survivors must be affirmed for the beauty they have acquired as they are enabled to live below the tree line, to flourish in an environment that contains ample soil and water and does not twist and tear at them.

Survivors of family abuse will never be towering oaks, but they can be guided and pruned to be the things of beauty to which they have been called. They can become saintly survivors.

Bibliography

Bellflower Center for Prevention of Child Abuse. 1987. "Nurturing Program." 11234 Bellflower Road, Cleveland, Ohio.

Bingham, Carol Findon, ed. 1986. *Doorway to Response: The Role of Clergy in Ministry with Battered Women.* Illinois Conference Churches.

Brueggemann, Walter. 1987. *Hope Within History.* Atlanta: John Knox Press.

Bussert, Joy M. K. 1986. *Battered Women: From a Theology of Suffering to an Ethic of Empowerment.* Division for Mission in the North American Lutheran Church in America.

Children's Defense Fund. 1988. *A Call for Action to Make Our Nation Safe for Children.* Washington, D.C.: CDF.

Clarke, Rita-Lou. 1986. *Pastoral Care of Battered Women.* Philadelphia: Westminster Press.

Coffin, William Sloane. 1981. Speech delivered to the Eighth Annual Assembly of the World YMCA, Geneva, Switzerland.

Daugherty, Lynn B. 1984. *Why Me? Help for Victims of Child Sexual Abuse (even if they are adults now).* Racine, Wis.: Mother Courage Press.

Diagnostic and Statistical Manual, vol. 3. 1980. Washington, D.C.: American Psychiatric Association.

Dobash, R. Emerson, and Russell Dobash. 1979. *Violence Against Wives: A Case Against the Patriarchy.* New York: Macmillan Publishing Co.

Erikson, Erik H. *Childhood and Society.* 1963. New York: W. W. Norton & Co.

Fox, Matthew. 1983. *Original Blessing.* Santa Fe, N. Mex.: Bear & Co.

Fortune, Marie M. 1983. *Sexual Violence: The Unmentionable Sin.* New York: Pilgrim Press.

———. 1987. *Keeping the Faith: Questions and Answers for the Abused.* New York: Harper & Row.

———. 1988. "Making Justice: Sources of Healing for Incest Survivors," *Working Together,* vol. 7, no. 4, pp. 5–6.

Garbarino, James, and Gwen Gilliam. 1980. *Understanding Abusive Families.* Lexington, Mass.: D. C. Heath & Co.

Gelles, Richard J. 1979. *Family Violence.* Beverly Hills, Calif.: Sage Publications.

—— and Claire Pedrick Corneﬂ. 1985. *Intimate Violence in Families.* Beverly Hills, Calif.: Sage Publications

Goldbrunner, Josef. 1964. *Holiness Is Wholeness.* Notre Dame, Ind.: University of Notre Dame Press.

Green, Bonnie L., John P. Wilson, and Jacob D. Lindy. 1981. "A Conceptual Framework for Post-Traumatic Stress Syndromes Among Survivor Groups," paper presented at the 33rd Institute on Hospital and Community Psychiatry, San Diego, Calif., September.

Greven, Philip. 1977. *The Protestant Temperament: Patterns of Child-Rearing, Religious Experience, and the Self in Early America.* New York: Alfred A. Knopf.

Harrison, Beverly Wildung. 1985. *Making the Connections: Essays in Feminist Social Ethics.* Boston: Beacon Press.

Helfer, Ray E. 1984. *Childhood Comes First: A Crash Course in Childhood for Adults.* East Lansing, Mich.: self-published.

Justice, Blair, and Rita Justice. 1976. *The Abusing Family.* New York: Human Sciences Press.

Kushner, Harold S. 1981. *When Bad Things Happen to Good People.* New York: Avon Books.

Leaman, Karen M. 1980. "Sexual Abuse: The Reactions of Child and Family," *Sexual Abuse of Children: Selected Readings.* Washington, D.C.: U.S. Department of Health and Human Services.

Leehan, James, and Laura Wilson. 1985. *Grown-Up Abused Children.* Springfield, Ill.: Charles C Thomas.

Lester, Andrew D. 1983. *Coping with Your Anger: A Christian Guide.* Philadelphia: Westminster Press.

Martin, Del. 1976. *Battered Wives.* San Francisco: Glide Publications.

Maslow, Abraham H. 1987. *Motivation and Personality.* New York: Harper & Row.

McGinnis, Kathleen, and James McGinnis. 1981. *Parenting for Peace and Justice.* Maryknoll, N.Y.: Orbis Books.

Nouwen, Henri J. M. 1975. *Reaching Out: The Three Movements of the Spiritual Life.* Garden City, N.Y.: Doubleday & Co.

President's Task Force on Victims of Crime. *Final Report*, December 1982.

Price-Martin, Barbara. 1987. "Theological Reflections on the Religious Dimension in Family Violence." *Working Together*, vol. 6, no. 3, pp. 2–4.

Richardson, Alan, ed. 1950. *A Theological Word Book of the Bible.* New York: Macmillan Co.

Simon, Sidney, and Suzanne Simon. 1987. "Forgiveness: Healing the Hurt," *VRI Journal*, pp. 3–5.

Spitzer, Julie Ringold. 1985. *Spousal Abuse in Rabbinic and Contemporary Judaism.* New York: National Federation of Temple Sisterhoods.

Steinmetz, Suzanne K. 1977. *The Cycle of Violence.* New York: Praeger Publishers.

Straus, Murray A., Susan K. Steinmetz, and Richard Gelles. 1981. *Behind Closed Doors: Violence in the American Family.* Garden City, N.Y.: Doubleday & Co.

Tavris, Carol. 1982. *Anger: The Misunderstood Emotion.* New York: Simon & Schuster.

Trible, Phyllis. 1978. *God and the Rhetoric of Sexuality.* Philadelphia: Fortress Press.

Walker, Lenore. 1979. *The Battered Woman.* New York: Harper & Row.

Wood, Frances E. 1988. "Mandatory 'Niceness': An Impediment to Justice and the Healing Process." *Working Together,* vol. 7, no. 6, pp. 1 and 2.

Printed in the United States
91951LV00005B/1-102/A